RAG DOLLS & HOW TO MAKE THEM

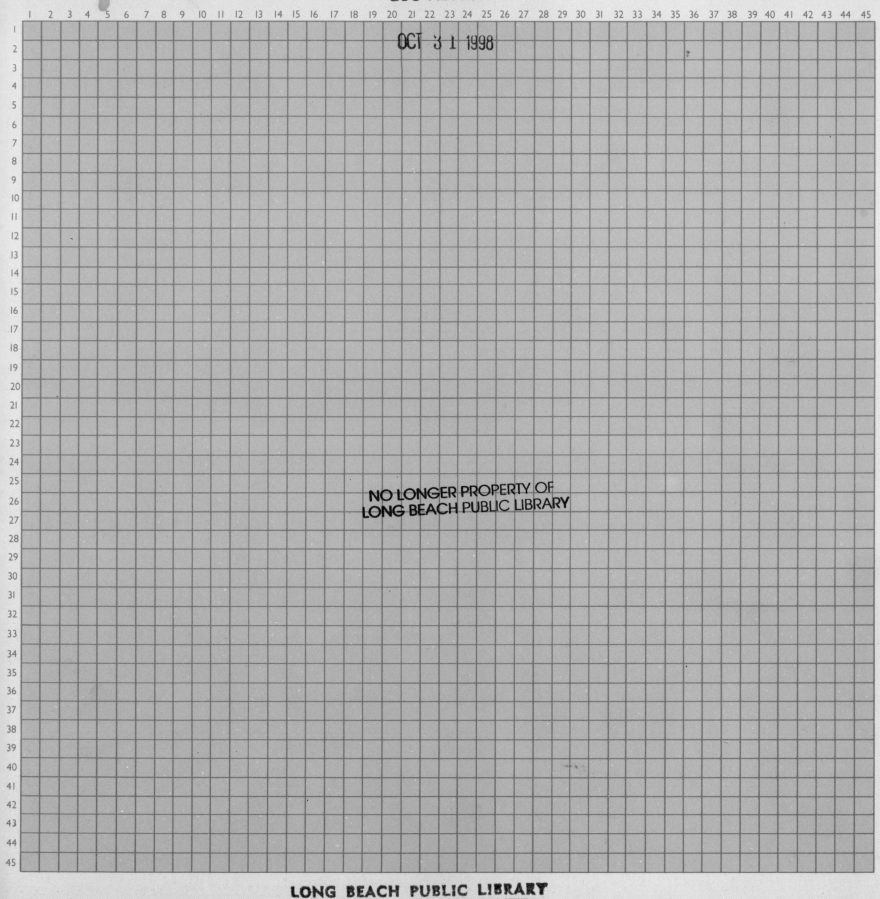

OCT 3 1 1998

RAG DOLLS & HOW TO MAKE THEM

EDITED BY DOROTHEA HALL

COURAGE
BOOKS

AN IMPRINT OF
RUNNING PRESS
PHILADELPHIA, PENNSYLVANIA

A QUARTO BOOK

Copyright © 1994 Quarto Publishing plc

All rights reserved under the Pan American and International Copyright
Conventions. First published in the United States of America in 1994 by Running
Press Book Publishers.

This book may not be reproduced in whole or in part in any form or by any means,
electronic or mechanical, including photocopying, recording, or by any information,
storage and retrieval system now known or hereafter invented, without written
permission from the publisher.

Canadian Representatives:
General Publishing Co., Ltd.
30 Lesmill Road, Don Mills
Ontario M3B 2T6

9 8 7 6 5 4 3 2 1
Digit on the right indicates the number of this printing.

ISBN 1-56138-352-X

Library of Congress Cataloging-in-Publication Number 93-85546

This book was designed and produced by
Quarto Publishing plc
The Old Brewery
6 Blundell Street
London N7 9BH

Senior editor Kate Kirby
Senior art editor Amanda Bakhtiar
Designer Debbie Mole
Illustrators Elsa Godfrey, Sally Launder, Rob Shone
Photographer Chas Wilder
Dollmakers Rona Kemp 4-23, 40-45, 86-117;
Melanie Williams 24-39, 46-85; Alicia Merrett 118-129
Consultant Janet Slingsby
Art director Moira Clinch

With special thanks to Sally Butler and Angela Faulkner

Typeset by West End Studios, Eastbourne
Manufactured in Hong Kong by Regent Publishing Services Ltd
Printed in Hong Kong by Lee-Fung Asco Printers Ltd

Published by Courage Books
An imprint of Running Press Book Publishers
125 South Twenty-second Street
Philadelphia, Pennsylvania 19103-4399.

$\mathcal{S}$AFETY GUIDELINES

1 When you buy fabrics, stuffing, and fittings, make sure that
they are from a reputable manufacturer who will have had to
satisfy legal requirements such as flammability, etc.

2 If you intend to make a toy doll for a small child or baby it
is safer not to use buttons, beads, or any other decoration
which can be pulled off and swallowed.

3 Do not under any circumstances use toxic paints, inks, or
dyes. Natural seed beads, especially imported ones, should be
avoided.

4 Joints should never be supported or attached with wire
which may eventually become loosened and pierce the fabric.

5 All commercial eye fastenings should be thoroughly
checked to make sure that they have the necessary safety
plates in place.

ONTENTS

BEFORE YOU START

PREPARATION OF FABRICS

With some of the bigger dolls you may wish to launder their clothes from time to time. Therefore, it is recommended that all new fabrics are washed and pressed before cutting out the pattern pieces. Gently hand wash in lukewarm soapy water (use mild soap flakes) and press between a clean towel to check for shrinkage and colorfastness before ironing dry.

AGEING NEW FABRICS

Character dolls such as the Old-fashioned dolls (page 58) are designed to look old and well loved. In order to achieve this effect, new fabrics should be steeped in strong tea before cutting out. Fill a large bowl with cold, strong tea and immerse all the fabrics required for the project. Leave for one or two minutes, remove and squeeze out the excess fluid. While still damp, press with a hot iron. This has the effect of scorching the fabric which also adds to the "antique" look.

TRACING ACTUAL-SIZE PATTERN PIECES

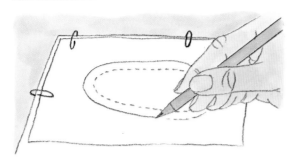

For·the pattern pieces which are given actual size, you can simply photocopy them from the book and cut out the copy. If a photocopying service is not available, make your own copy using tracing paper. Place the tracing paper on top of your chosen pattern, secure the edges firmly with paper clips,

and draw with a pencil around the pattern outline. Use a ruler for all straight lines. Copy all marks and information and cut out your traced pattern piece using general-purpose scissors. (For pattern pieces that need to be enlarged see the box opposite.)

CUTTING OUT PATTERN PIECES

When you have cut out all the paper pattern pieces for your chosen project and marked and labeled them, the next step is to follow the fabric cutting layout. First determine how the fabric has been folded, if at all. You will notice, in some instances, that the fabric has been folded leaving a layer of single fabric to one side.

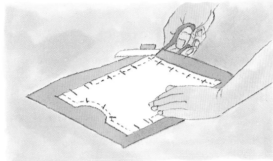

1 Working on a flat surface, arrange your pattern pieces on the appropriate fabric as shown in the diagram. Pin them in place, pinning the straight grain line first. Cut out using sharp dressmaker's scissors.

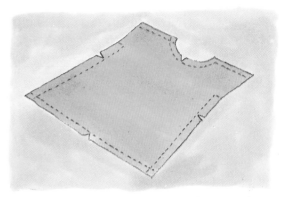

2 Clip into the seam line to show the center front (CF) and center back (CB) on the appropriate pattern pieces. Transfer balance marks, darts, and on some doll patterns the face and shoe details, using dressmaker's carbon paper.

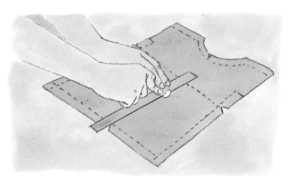

3 To trace the marks, place the waxed side of the carbon paper to the wrong side of the fabric – you may have to remove a few pins. Trace the markings on with a tracing wheel and ruler using short, firm strokes.

4 When transferring face and shoe details, work freehand with the carbon paper placed waxed side to the right side of the fabric, underneath your tracing. Use a soft pencil or empty ballpoint pen for tracing.

ENLARGING PAPER PATTERN PIECES

The half-size pattern pieces given for some of the projects in this book need to be enlarged before you can pin the pattern pieces onto the fabric. The easiest method is to use a photocopier.

Using a photocopier: set the machine to enlarge the copy by 200% then photocopy the required pattern pieces. Once enlarged, cut out the paper pattern pieces and pin them onto the fabric.

USING THE GRID METHOD

If a photocopier is not available, then the pattern pieces can be enlarged using the grids supplied with this book.

1 Trace off the small grid (A) which you will find at the beginning of this book.

2 Place the traced-off grid on top of the pattern pieces you wish to enlarge and trace them off.

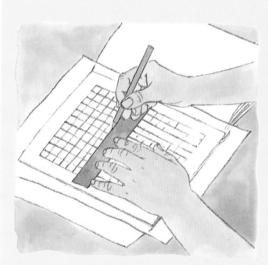

3 On a separate sheet of paper, trace off the large grid (B) which you will find at the back of this book.

4 The pattern pieces traced off onto the grid. Note all construction points and information have been transcribed.

Using grid A as a point of reference, mark on grid B the points where the outline of the pattern crosses the grid lines then join up these marks to complete the pattern shapes. Add all construction points and information, then cut out the paper pattern pieces and pin them to the fabric.

MACHINE STITCHING

Before making the dolls, it is advisable to check the stitch on a spare piece of the fabric you have chosen. For ordinary seams and most sewing situations, straight stitch lengths range from 10-15 stitches per 1in. For gathering, the length ranges from 6-9 stitches per 1in. And for seams on lightweight fabrics, use a finer stitch ranging from 16-24 stitches per 1in. Check the tension and adjust, if necessary. The correct tension should show the link formed with each stitch to lie halfway between the fabric layers – so the stitching will look the same on both sides of the fabric.

SEAMS

Unless otherwise stated within a project, most seams used throughout the book are plain open seams which are first stitched, trimmed back, and then clipped or notched, depending on the location and the type of fabric used.

1 Machine (or hand) stitch the seam, and then trim the seam allowance from ½in to ¼in or as instructed. The fabric is cut away to reduce bulk, especially necessary for making dolls.

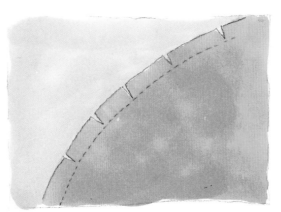

2 Convex or outward curved seams should then be clipped. Cut small slits into the seam allowance. These will spread out and allow the edge to lie flat when finished.

3 Notches are V-shaped wedges which are cut out from concave or inward seams to allow the two edges of the V to come together when the seam is turned inside and thus reduce bulk.

PATTERN PIECE NOTATION

All the patterns used within the book have markings that are indispensable to accurate cutting out and the subsequent construction of a project. The markings are defined as follows:

- **Cutting line:** heavy outline on a pattern piece.

  ─────────────

- **Seam line:** Indicated by a dashed line usually positioned ½in inside the cutting line, but it does vary with certain projects.

  ─ ─ ─ ─ ─ ─

- **Balance marks:** denoted by straight lines, are also construction points used for accurate joining of pieces and may be used on very small pattern pieces for clarity or on others where there are additional marks that would otherwise be confusing.

- **Center front, center back:** indicated by a seam line or fold line clearly labeled with CF or CB. (This notation appears on only some pattern pieces.)

- **Grain line:** straight line ending with arrowheads means "place on straight grain of fabric."

- **Place-on-fold bracket:** grain line marking with directional arrows means the outline should be placed exactly on the folded edge of the fabric.

  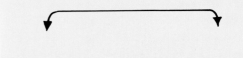

- **Darts:** broken (stitching) lines meet at a center point.

THE WORKBASKET

The basic equipment needed for making cloth dolls is simple and inexpensive and can be bought from most needlework and craft stores, if you don't already have the items in your workbasket.

NEEDLES

- **Sharps** (sizes 5-10) are round-eyed and sharp-pointed and are used for all hand sewing with general-purpose sewing thread or tacking cotton.
- **Crewel** needles (sizes 1-10) have sharp points and long oval eyes and are used for all forms of fine to medium-weight embroidery using either six-stranded embroidery thread or single threads, such as coton à broder and pearl threads.
- **Chenille** needles (sizes 18-24) are similar to crewel needles but are much bigger and stronger.

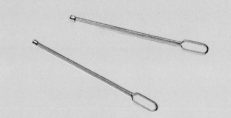

- **Bodkin** (usually one size) This is a large oval-eyed round-ended needle useful for working with coarse yarns and fabrics.
- **Elastic threader** (usually one size) is a flat, large-eyed needle with a round point used for threading elastic or narrow ribbon or tape through a casing.

THREADS

- **General-purpose sewing threads** are available in cotton or cotton/polyester. They are produced in a wide range of colors, and it should be possible to match any fabric.

- **Strong thread** or buttonhole thread is a tightly twisted single thread with a lustrous finish. It is useful for stitching doll joints that require a flexible shank, for example.
- **Six-stranded embroidery thread** is a loosely-twisted mercerized cotton used for surface embroidery. Produced in a vast array of colors, it can be split and used in varying thicknesses to give lighter or more solid effects.
- **Coton à broder** is a lightly twisted single thread available in a range of colors.
- **Pearl cotton** is a tightly twisted single thread available in a variety of thicknesses and colors.
- **Tacking thread** is a loosely twisted cotton thread (usually white) used for the stitching which temporarily holds together fabric layers.
- **Shirring elastic** or elastic thread: Nylon/cotton wrapped thread. Stretchy and reasonably thick, it is used for shirring on the sewing machine, and is wound on to the bobbin only.
- **Scissors** It is useful to have a pair of dressmaker's shears for cutting fabric; a pair of sharp-pointed embroidery scissors for snipping into seams and a pair of general purpose scissors for cutting paper.

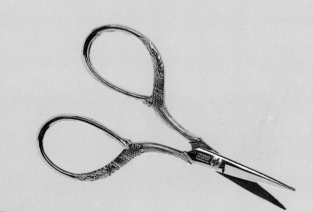

- **Sewing machine** A sewing machine is useful for making up items, especially on larger projects where it will give a stronger seam and quicker results.

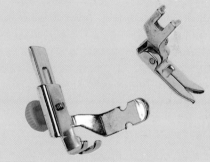

- **Knitting needle** A strong knitting needle is the perfect tool for helping to stuff cloth dolls. Use the blunt end for pushing in the stuffing and use the pointed end carefully for getting into corners.
- **Fray check** is a quick-drying sealant that can be applied to the raw edges of fabric to stop them fraying.
- **Dressmaker's carbon paper** is usually sold in packs of different colors. The darker tones are used to transfer marks or motifs to light-colored fabrics, while lighter shades are used for darker-colored fabrics.
- **Tracing wheel**, in appearance rather like a pastry wheel, this wheeled marking gauge enables the speedy transition of pattern marks to fabric.
- **Air-vanishing pencil**, as its name implies, is a marking pencil with a temporary effect as the marks will disappear after a short while.
- **Additional items include:** a thermostatically controlled steam iron – ideal for this type of craftwork; fine, stainless steel dressmaker's pins; a thimble; tape measure; ruler and pencil; fabric adhesive.

TYPES OF BODY

Cloth dolls fall into certain categories according to the type of body they have. Some small dolls, for example, are made from just two pieces of fabric while others are made from several; some are flat and others are well-rounded.

There are dolls with fixed limbs and neck like the Pocket Dolls on page 14, which are eminently suitable for the tiny hands of babies and small children. Others, such as the Amish-style Dolls, page 46, have stitched joints which makes them semi-flexible and can be dressed and undressed more easily. Some of the bigger dolls have shank joints or bead joints, see pages 86 and 118, which allow their limbs to swing easily. Other features such as angled and straight-stitched leg joints enable dolls to balance when sitting down. The information given in the following pages explains in detail the different features that have been used in the construction of the dolls.

the smaller sizes make ideal hand toys for babies and small children made simply from gingham or terrycloth fabric.

Method Cut out the doll pattern from your chosen fabric allowing a ½in seam allowance all round. Machine stitch around leaving an opening at the top of the head. Trim the seam by half, snip into the neck, between the limbs and into the curved seam, and turn through. Lightly stuff so that the doll remains flat but slightly rounded and flexible. Slip stitch the opening to close.

Combined head and body dolls have separate limbs which can be attached with either an angled or straight seam depending on the shape of the body. The body may also be curved at the waist to give a female shape.

around the shape, reinforcing the neck and shoulder seam with a second row of stitching. Clip into the curves and turn through. Stuff to give a soft, flexible finish and slip stitch the opening to close. Attach the limbs by oversewing them to the body, as instructed.

Straight-stitched joints (arms and legs) may be stitched through on a combined body and limb doll to give a little more flexibility, or separate limbs can be inserted or oversewn to the straight sides of the body.

Combined head, body and limbs is the simplest doll construction involving just two sections of fabric cut out in the shape of a doll, see Pocket Dolls page 14. This type of doll can be any size but

Method Decide on the technique for attaching the limbs of your doll and whether you want a waisted female shape, and then cut out the combined head and body pattern from double fabric. Leaving an opening in the side for turning through, stitch

Method On a combined body and limb doll, simply backstitch the top arm/shoulder and leg joints stitching through all layers. Where individual limbs are attached, make the limbs as instructed and pin them in place to the body. Using strong thread and fairly small stitches, firmly overcast each limb working with the back of the doll uppermost.

Angle-stitched joints give a little more sophistication to the anatomical shape of the doll. Where both the body and limbs are even slightly angled, the limbs will hang naturally downwards but point outwards. Angle-stitched legs will also give the doll a broader base to balance on when sitting down.

Method The technique is generally the same as for straight-stitched joints but some construction methods may leave openings in the body for the stuffed limbs to be inserted and then stitched through all four layers (body and limbs) using backstitch to secure them. In this case, the limbs are left unstitched after stuffing.

Shank joints made by wrapping around several connecting stitches to form a shank, are very strong and offer the most flexibility for both arms and legs. Used mainly on bigger dolls, shank leg joints will enable the doll to sit in a well-balanced position.

Method This is similar to making a button shank. Several connecting threads are taken across from the body to the limb; then the threads are wrapped around to form a shank, finishing off by taking the needle through the body. Use strong thread to ensure a long-lasting joint.

Tubular body forms the lower part of the doll and enables it to stand on a flat circular base in order to display, for example, an ethnic-style costume. The hollow card tube is weighted to help keep the doll upright.

Method A card circular base is first attached to one end of the empty tube. Dried beans, or other suitable fillings, are then put inside and a card lid attached. The tube is then inserted into the fabric body where the head and shoulders have already been stuffed. The lower edge of the fabric is gathered over the bottom of the tube and separate arms oversewn in place to complete the body.

Bead joints are very decorative and also give flexibility to the knee and elbow joints. The size of the beads should be in proportion to the size of the limbs, and the central hole should be big enough to allow the chosen fabric to be threaded through.

Method Choose the color of bead to complement the fabric of your doll. Beginning with the lower part of the limb (the foot or the hand), stuff firmly, as instructed, as far as the knee or elbow joint and then thread on the bead. Push the bead down firmly and continue stuffing the upper part of the limb. Oversew the opening to close. Attach the arms and legs to the doll's body following the instructions given.

Three-dimensional body and limbs involves stitching together several pattern pieces to make a separate head, body, arms, and legs. These are then stuffed firmly, sometimes quite hard, and with a well-rounded finish. The doll is usually assembled with a forward projecting face and feet and with defined fingers.

Method The individual pattern pieces are cut out and stitched in the usual way (the body and upper limbs can be made from a contrasting patterned fabric). The different parts are then stuffed using a knitting needle to push the stuffing well in. To give shape to the face, a dart on the front head section forms the chin. The neck of the stuffed head is inserted into the stuffed body and oversewn around the base of the neck. The legs and arms are pleated at the top edge, placing the seams in the center, before securing them to the body. This ensures that the feet and the profile of the hands point forward. The fingers are then defined with rows of backstitching.

Double-headed body is used for the Upside-down Doll, see page 40, where the doll's long skirt is also "double" and hides the second doll when the opposite doll is held in an upright position.

Method The combined pattern of a body with a head at each end (reversed at the waist) is cut out, stitched and stuffed in the usual way. Two sets of arms are also made and are attached at the shoulders with shank joints. The doll has no legs.

FACES AND HAIR

Painted face and eyes

Before a doll is given clothes, its character is firmly established with the addition of the face and hair. Features can vary enormously from a few embroidered lines, as on the Rabbit Pocket Doll, page 22, to the multicolored effect of the Painted Doll, page 24.

Hair can be as simple as knotted lengths of raffia, as for the Angel on my pillow Doll on page 86, or as elaborate as the Classic Doll's coiffure, page 108. The following information lists the variety of styles and techniques that have been used within the book, but with a little imagination, you can easily combine and adapt these techniques to create your own unique dolls.

FACES

Embroidery usually involves stitching the features directly onto the face with colored embroidery threads and using a variety of embroidery stitches such as satin and stem stitch and French knots.

Method Using either a freehand pencil line or dressmaker's carbon paper, transfer the features from the pattern to the right side of the fabric – ideally before the head is finished. Work the embroidery after stuffing, strengthening any faint lines with a pencil. Begin by inserting the needle some distance away from the face detail, leaving a short thread hanging. Secure it at the first stitch and trim back later. Do the same in reverse for finishing. (See the stitch glossary).

Appliqué is the technique whereby the features are cut out from non-fraying fabric and applied to the face with fabric adhesive, hemstitching, or decorative embroidery stitches.

Method As a guideline, transfer the simple outline of the features to the fabric as for "Embroidery." Cut out the features from a non-fraying fabric like felt, and use fabric adhesive to glue them in place. Shapes can then be hemstitched around using a matching thread and/or decoratively embroidered with colored threads. Eyes and cheek circles, for example, can be overstitched with contrasting crossed stitches.

Soft sculpture, as its name implies, involves pulling stitches down into the filling to form features on the doll's face.

Method In order to give depth to the features, the face fabric should not be too stiff nor the stuffing too hard. Using an air-vanishing pencil, transfer guidelines to the face before stitching. With matching strong (or double) thread in a long needle, insert the needle from the back of the stuffed head, make a small stitch and return the needle to the back pulling the thread tight. Continue in this way until you have the desired feature effect, finishing off at the back underneath the hair.

Painting can include using different colored fabric paints, fabric dyes, or water-soluble crayons to suggest features and hair.

Method Fabric paints and dyes can be watered down to give varying tones and shades. Practice first on spare fabric with different-sized brushes, colors, and shaded effects. Transfer guidelines, using an air-vanishing pencil, to the stuffed head and paint directly on the fabric. Allow the paint to dry between applications and remember to clean brushes well before mixing new colors.

Waterproof markers and cosmetic blushers: Waterproof markers (available in a variety of colors) can be used successfully to "draw" in the features. Cosmetic blushers are ideal for suggesting a "blush" on the cheeks of a doll.

Plastic safety eyes and drawn-on features

Raffia hair

Bead eyes, embroidered nose, and mouth

Soft sculpture face   *Appliqued features*   *Embroidered face and hair*

Method Waterproof markers are ideal for suggesting features, either as a simple outline or as a "feathered" line, as in eyebrows, for example. Following a guideline, which can be made with an ordinary or air-vanishing pencil, draw directly onto the stuffed face with the appropriate marker. For a very quick effect, mouths and eyebrows can be suggested with a single line, and nostrils, freckles, and even eyes with dots.

Buttons, beads, and safety eyes can all be used to create charming faces. Commercially bought toy eyes have a safety device to lock them in place.

Method Buttons and beads can be used for eyes and cheeks. Secure very firmly and do not use on dolls designed as toys for babies or young children. For readymade toy eyes, follow the manufacturer's instructions.

HAIR

Yarn is available in a great variety of colors and thicknesses from bulky knitting to two-ply embroidery yarn. It can be applied to the head in stitched hanks to be plaited or tied in bunches, or applied in tight curls. Shorter strands can be

unraveled for a tousled look. Thick yarn is particularly good for larger dolls.

Method For either long or short hair, the yarn is first cut into lengths, laid over a piece of fabric tape and stitched to it. The tape is then stitched or glued to the head, and the strands are neatly arranged over the head. Depending on the style, the yarn can be stuck under the hairline around the face and around the neckline before finishing in braids, etc. Additional layers may be applied on top.

Embroidery threads offer a wide range of colors, thicknesses, and textures. They can be mixed in the needle and stitched directly through the fabric on the head. The scale of these threads is especially good for smaller dolls.

Method One of the most attractive styles uses loop stitch. This is worked all over the head to give a short, curly effect. Using stranded floss or heavy pearl cotton in the needle (in mixed, random-dyed or a single color), work two backstitches; allow the first stitch to remain as a loop (its size determining the depth of the hair) and make the second stitch in the same place but pull this one firmly through to secure the loop. The loops can be left as curls or cut for a spiky effect.

Rayon tubular cord is beautifully soft and hangs well. It is fairly narrow, less than ⅛in across, is available in several colors, and can be used in a similar way to yarn.

Method Wind the cord around two individual pieces of cardboard (each one cut to the hair length required measured from the center parting). Then stitch the loops at one end to secure them. Slide each set of loops off the cardboard and neatly stitch the two secured ends together. Stitch to the center of the doll's head and finish as for yarn.

Raffia is available in a wide choice of colors and in several thicknesses. For "hair," choose the wider variety where coverage is a consideration. Although raffia has a delightful appeal, it should not be used on dolls for small children or babies who may put it in their mouths.

Method Cut the raffia into uneven lengths, roughly 5in long, depending on the size of the doll, and with a large chenille needle, thread each length through the head fabric. Secure with a square knot. Continue to cover the head working around the face, over the back of the head and down the neckline. Space the knots about ½in apart.

Fabric strips can be given a particularly charming, homespun effect, especially with country-style ginghams, checks, and plaids. The fabric is cut into narrow widths and the edges left to ravel before the strips are knotted into the doll's head.

Method Strips of fabric about ½in wide are cut, or torn, and then shortened into 4in lengths (depending on the size of the doll). Using an elastic threader, or large bodkin, thread the strips through the doll's head making the "stitch" about ⅜in wide. Tie each length into a square knot and leave the edges to ravel.

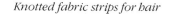
Knotted fabric strips for hair

Buttons for eyes

POCKET DOLLS ARE QUICK AND EASY TO MAKE, AND YOU CAN PERSONALIZE THEM TO SUIT THE RECIPIENT. USE ONE OF THE IDEAS HERE OR DEVELOP YOUR OWN DESIGNS.

POCKET DOLLS

Just two basic pattern pieces are needed to make these versatile pocket dolls. Choose plain fabric for realistic dolls or let your imagination run riot and use patterned material for unusual, fun effects. Pocket dolls are so simple and inexpensive to make that you can afford to experiment! A washable terrycloth doll is just right for a baby, while older children will love dolls dressed in their favorite team's uniform.

MATERIALS

TWIN DOLLS

(measure 9in high)

- 18in of 36in-wide lightweight muslin for the two bodies
- 4in of 10in-wide fur fabric for the hair
- Synthetic stuffing or kapok
- Waterproof felt-tipped pens (red and black) for the face details
- Pink blusher for the cheeks
- Felt scraps for the eyes
- 9in of 36in-wide printed cotton for the dress and overalls
- Fabric glue
- 14in of grosgrain ribbon for boy's suspenders and bowtie
- Two buttons, about ⅜in across, for boy's overalls
- 18in of narrow ribbon for the girl's hair
- 10in of round elastic for the dress and overalls

CHECKERED BOY

(measures 9in high)

- 12in × 18in of check cotton fabric for the body
- 8in × 12in of contrasting cotton fabric for the overalls
- Scraps of third contrasting fabric for the hair
- Synthetic stuffing or kapok
- 10in of ⅝in-wide grosgrain ribbon for the suspenders
- Two small buttons, about ⅜in across
- 4in of round elastic
- Large-eyed chenille needle or bodkin

Fresh cotton prints and trimmings for the twins.

Crisp checks for the body and a contrasting cotton for the overalls make for a smart "checkered boy."

GINGHAM GIRL

(measures 9in high)

- 12in × 18in of cotton fabric, such as lawn for body
- Synthetic stuffing or kapok
- 1oz skein of black yarn for the hair
- Scraps of black and red felt for the eyes and mouth
- 18in of ¼in-wide ribbon for the hair
- 6in × 16in of gingham check for the dress
- 6in of round elastic for the dress
- Fabric glue
- Black waterproof felt-tip pen

RABBIT

(measures 9in high)

- 12in × 24in of blue brushed cotton for the body
- 6in × 22in of a contrasting cotton for the dress and the inner ears
- Scraps of blue felt for the eyes
- Synthetic stuffing or kapok
- Blue stranded embroidery floss for the features
- 6in of round elastic
- Fabric glue

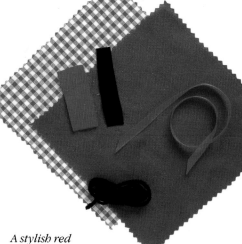

*A stylish red
and white check
has been chosen for
the little gingham girl.*

*Soft brushed cotton body with contrasting polkadot
cotton print for the dress and ears make for a
sweet little rabbit. Felt and embroidery thread
are used for the facial features.*

BRIDE

(measures 9in high)

- 12in × 18in of muslin for the body
- 1oz of yarn for the hair
- Synthetic stuffing or kapok
- Fine felt-tipped pens (red and black) and blusher for the face
- 1yd of 5in-wide lace, with one bound edge, for the dress
- 1yd of 5in-wide lace for the veil
- 7in of ½in-wide lace for the collar band
- 18in of ⅜in-wide lace for the wrists
- Three satin ribbon flowers
- 14in of round elastic

ANGEL

(measures 9in high)

- 12in × 18in of muslin for the body
- Two blue beads for the eyes
- 10in of narrow gold cord for the hair
- 1oz of ⅛in-wide cream nylon knitting ribbon for the hair
- Synthetic stuffing or kapok
- Blue stranded embroidery floss for the face details
- 10in × 20in of white cotton fabric for the dress
- 1yd of gold trim, such as braid, for dress
- 8in × 12in of white organza for the wings
- Gold sequins to decorate the wings and hair
- 1yd of ½in-wide gold ribbon for the neck and wings
- Six white pipecleaners for the wings
- Fabric glue

*The bride wears satin rosebuds and
different widths of lace.*

*The pocket angel is made of scraps of
ribbon, gold cord, braid, and a star-
patterned fabric.*

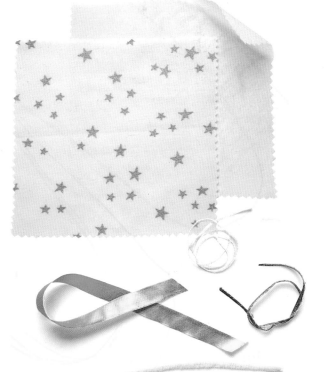

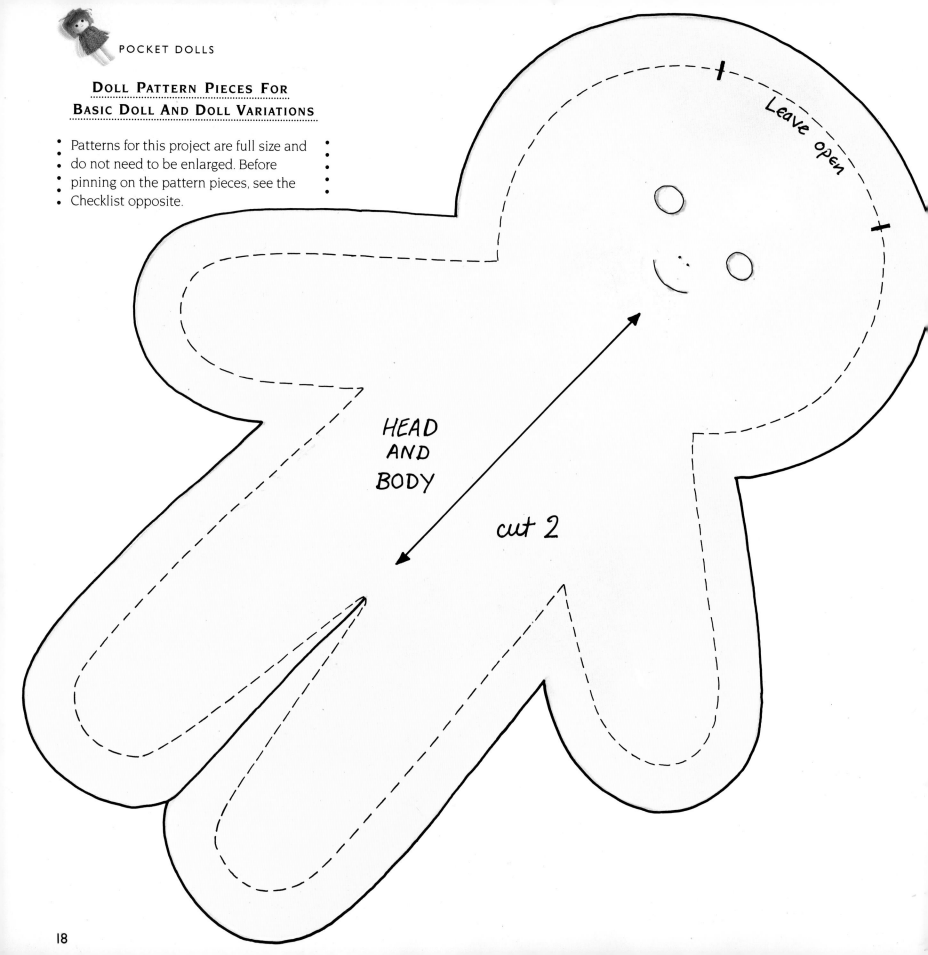

DOLL PATTERN PIECES FOR
BASIC DOLL AND DOLL VARIATIONS

Patterns for this project are full size and do not need to be enlarged. Before pinning on the pattern pieces, see the Checklist opposite.

Leave open

HEAD
AND
BODY

cut 2

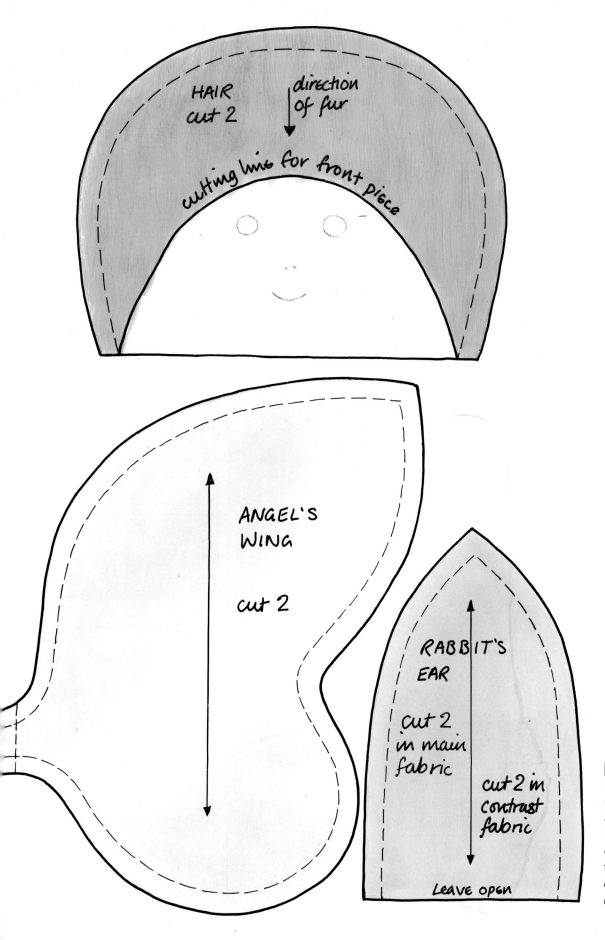

HAIR
cut 2

direction
of fur

cutting line for front piece

ANGEL'S
WING

cut 2

RABBIT'S
EAR

cut 2
in main
fabric

cut 2 in
contrast
fabric

Leave open

CHECKLIST

- Trace off the outline of the actual size pattern pieces. Transfer all marks and cut out, see pages 6-7.
- Wash and press the main fabrics to test for shrinkage and colourfastness.
- Cut out the required number for each pattern piece from the correct fabric.
- Set your sewing machine to the required stitch, check the length and tension and do a test run on your chosen fabric, see page 8.
- Seam allowances are included on all the doll body patterns. Stitch and trim back to ¼in, snip into curved seams and press open, see page 8. Note that individual seam allowances may vary for some of the alternative details such as clothes and the fabric fur hair.

Twin dolls: cutting layout for fur fabric

TWIN DOLLS ~
HEAD AND BODY

1 With the right sides facing, pin, baste, and machine stitch around the body, leaving the seam open as indicated on the pattern. Trim the seam allowance and clip the seam at the neck, arms, and in between the legs. Turn right side out. Stuff evenly, using a large knitting needle to help push the filling in place. Turn in the seam allowance and overcast the opening to close. Make the second doll in exactly the same way.

HAIR

2 For each doll, pin together one front and one back hair piece with the right sides facing, and machine stitch around the outer curved edge only. Turn right side out and glue in place. Cut the boy's hair ¼in shorter around the face. Tie the narrow ribbon in a decorative bow and sew to the center of the girl's hair.

FACE

3 For the eyes, cut four ¼in circles out of felt and glue two to each face. Suggest the nose and mouth with fine felt-tipped pens, and the cheeks with a light dusting of blusher.

CLOTHING PATTERN PIECES FOR
BASIC CLOTHING AND
CLOTHING VARIATIONS

· Patterns for this project are full size and do not need to be enlarged. Tape the two dress pattern pieces together before cutting the fabric. Before pinning on the pattern pieces, see the Checklist on page 19.

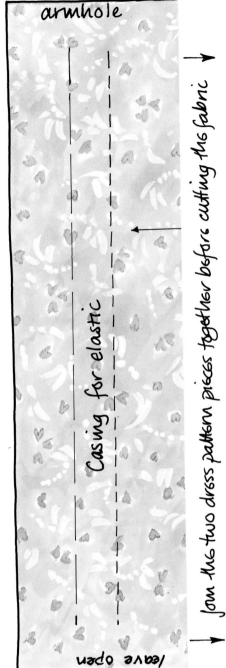

armhole

Casing for elastic

leave open

Join the two dress pattern pieces together before cutting the fabric

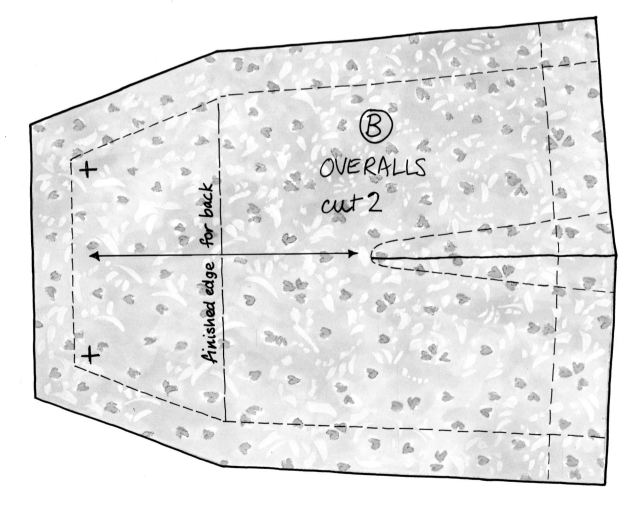

Ⓑ
OVERALLS
cut 2

finished edge for back

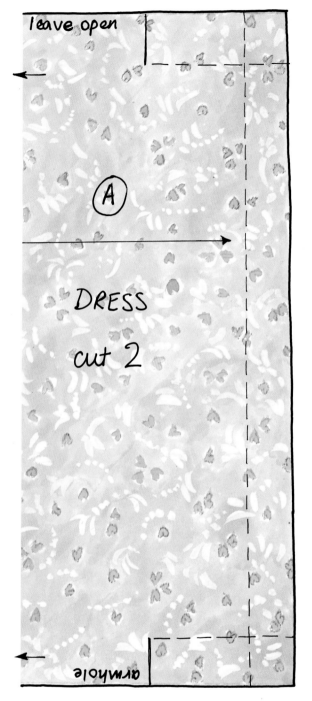

leave open

(A)

DRESS

cut 2

armhole

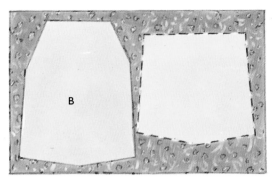

Cutting layout for basic overalls/trousers and variations

Fold

A

Cutting layout for basic dress and dress variations

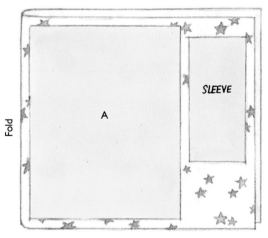

Fold

A

SLEEVE

Cutting layout for angel's dress

TWIN GIRL'S DRESS

1 Pin the two dress pieces together with the right sides facing, and machine stitch the side seams from the hem to the notch marked. Press the seam open. Make narrow double hems on each armhole opening and machine stitch to secure.

2 On the front and back pieces of the dress, make a ½in double turning along the neck edge to form a casing. Thread the elastic through both casings to fit the neck and overcast the ends together. Pin and machine stitch a ¼in hem along the bottom of the dress to finish.

TWIN BOY'S OVERALLS

3 On the pants front piece, pin and machine stitch a narrow hem, first along the side edges and then across the top of the bib, and also along the waistline of the pants back piece.

4 With the right sides facing, machine stitch the back and front pieces together along the sides and around the inner leg seams. Clip the seam allowance between the legs after sewing. Turn up the leg hems to the required length and stitch.

5 From the ribbon, cut two straps each 5in long and hand sew them to each side of the front bib on the wrong side. Attach the two small buttons on top. Cross the straps at the back and secure with back stitch just below the stitchline. Thread the elastic through the hem at the back waistline, adjust the length for a correct fit and overcast the ends to hold.

BOY'S BOWTIE

6 Make the bowtie from the remaining ribbon by folding it, as shown, and tightly tying around the center with sewing thread. Glue or sew it in place on the boy's neck.

CHECKERED BOY ~ BODY AND CLOTHES

1 Make the doll from the check cotton fabric and the overalls from a contrasting fabric (see the recommended materials list on page 16). Follow step 1, page 19 and steps 3-5, pages 21-22.

HAIR

2 Cut several lengths of fabric about 4in long by ⅜in wide. With a length of fabric in the chenille needle or bodkin, make a small stitch and pull it through the fabric on top of the doll's head. Tie with a square knot and repeat at random over the top of the head, as shown.

GINGHAM GIRL ~ BODY AND CLOTHES

1 Following the instructions given on page 19, step 1, make the doll from the cotton fabric as suggested (for recommended materials, see page 16).

2 Cut two ⅜in circles from the black felt for the eyes and a ⅝in-wide crescent from the red felt for the mouth. Glue these in place and then suggest the nose with a fine felt-tipped pen.

3 For the bangs, cut several 6in lengths of yarn and tie them together in the center. Glue this to the top of the head with the cut ends falling forward. Cut the remaining yarn into 18in lengths and,

again, tie around the center with a separate length of yarn. Glue the center of the tied strands to the top of the head, making the tying strand the center parting. Glue also around the hairline of the face and neck. Plait the loose strands at the sides of the head; cut the ribbon in half and tie around to secure the ends of the braids. Trim the ends to finish.

4 Make the dress from the gingham check following the instructions given on page 21, steps 1 and 2.

RABBIT DOLL ~ BODY AND CLOTHES

1 Make the doll and clothes following the materials list on page 16 and the instructions given on page 19, step 1 and page 21, steps 1 and 2. Cut two ¼in circles from the blue felt for the eyes and glue them in place. Embroider the nose and whiskers using long straight stitches.

2 Pin the four ear pieces together using one main and one contrasting fabric piece for each ear and with right sides facing. Machine stitch around each curved edge. Turn right side out. Turn in the seam allowance at the opening and overcast the edges together by hand. Pin the ears in position on top of the head folding the outer edges inward and hemstitch in place.

BRIDE ~
BODY AND CLOTHES

1 Make the doll from muslin following the materials list on page 17 and the instructions given on page 19, step 1. Draw the face using the black pen for the nose and suggest the cheeks with a light dusting of blusher.

2 To make the hair, cut a long length of yarn and wind it around a ruler. Backstitch along the top edge to hold the loops together. Slip the loops off the ruler and hemstitch in place in rows across the head beginning at the base of the neck. Repeat until the head is completely filled. For smaller curls, wind the yarn around a pencil.

3 Cut the dress lace in half to make a separate skirt and top. Cut 8in of elastic for the waist and 6in for the neck. Thread the 8in of elastic through the binding on one of the pieces of lace and knot the ends together. Fit this skirt on the doll with a center back opening. Thread the other piece of elastic through the remaining lace to make the top of the dress. On this piece, join the raw edges together with a line of running stitches and then pull them up to make a finished shoulder width of about 2in. Repeat on the opposite shoulder.

4 Sew the ½in-wide lace around the neck by hand and glue one of the flowers to the center front. Cut the ⅜in-wide lace in two and tie around each wrist. Gather the unfinished edge of the veil lace by machine and hand sew it to the top of the head in a semicircle and stitch two flowers in each corner.

ANGEL ~
BODY AND CLOTHES

1 Make the doll from the muslin following the materials list on page 17 and the instructions given on page 19, step 1.

2 For the hair, wind the knitting ribbon around a piece of cardboard 5in deep, dividing it into two separate skeins. Tie each skein firmly around one end, and remove from the board. Overcast the two skeins to the center of the head so that they fall to each side of the face. Glue along the hairline and secure with the narrow gold cord around the head. Hold the cord in place by stitching a sequin to the center part, as shown. For the eyes, hand sew the two small beads in place and then, using one strand of embroidery thread, make a straight stitch for the nose and a French knot for the mouth.

3 To make the long dress with sleeves, use the white cotton fabric and follow the dress instructions given on page 21, step 1 and 2, but first extend the length of the dress to 6½in and, for the sleeves, cut two strips 2½in × 5¼in from the same fabric.

4 Using the wing pattern as a template, twist to join three pipecleaners together and mold to the required shape. Repeat for the second wing. Cut two wings from the organza and glue the pipecleaners in place. Glue the sequins to decorate the top half of each wing. Overcast the wings together at the center point and then stitch them to the center back of the doll. Tie the remaining ½in-wide ribbon in a bow and stitch it over the join.

OTHER POCKET DOLL VARIATIONS

A pocket ballerina made from cotton, pink satin, and stiffened net.

Green organza, blue satin, and shredded paper are used for this charming mermaid.

This terrycloth baby wears a lace-trimmed night cap.

23

NO-SEW CLOTHES MAKE THIS

PAINTED DOLL THE IDEAL PROJECT

FOR LESS EXPERIENCED

NEEDLEWORKERS AND FOR

CHILDREN EAGER TO LEND A

HELPING HAND.

FABRIC-PAINTED DOLL

Sew and stuff a very simple body, then use fabric paints to create the clothes, face, hair, and shoes of your choice. Fabric paints are now available in a very wide choice of colors and textures so you will be able to achieve an exciting variety of effects.

Metallic gold and silver paints will produce a stunning Christmas angel, for example – or paints with a raised, bead-like texture can be used for unusual jewelry or hair effects.

MATERIALS

DOLL (measures 10½in high)

- 16in × 10in of lightweight muslin for the body
- Synthetic stuffing or kapok
- Fabric paints in the colors of your choice (blues, pinks, and greens are suitable for traditional garments: browns for hair)
- Paintbrushes in varying sizes (small to medium)
- Pencil

PANTALOONS

- 10in × 8in of lightweight white cotton fabric for the pantaloons
- 12in of lace trim

Muslin, fine white cotton, and lace trim for the body and clothes.

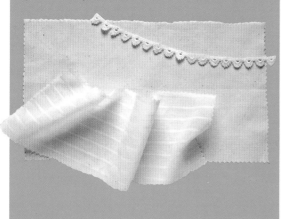

DOLL PATTERN PIECES

Patterns for this project are full size and do not need to be enlarged. Before pinning on the pattern pieces, see the Checklist opposite.

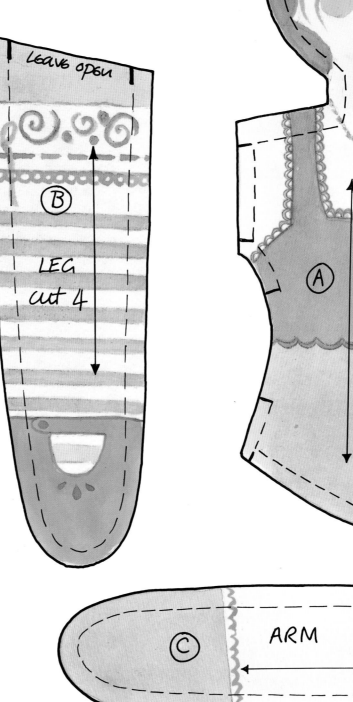

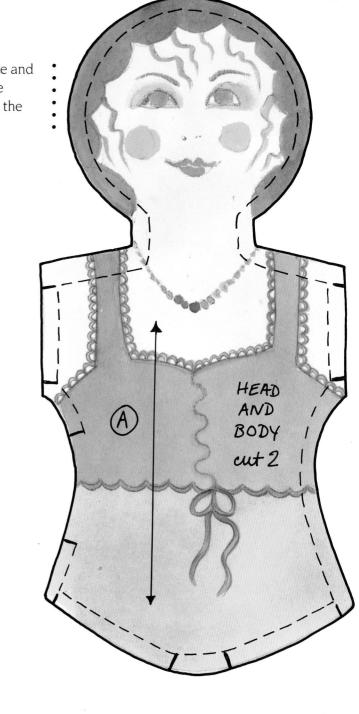

Leave open

Ⓑ LEG cut 4

HEAD AND BODY cut 2

Ⓐ

Ⓒ ARM cut 4

Leave open

CHECKLIST

- Trace off the outline of the actual size pattern pieces, transfer all marks and cut out, see pages 6-7.
- Wash and press all main fabrics to test for shrinkage and colorfastness, see page 6.
- Cut out the required number for each pattern piece from the appropriate fabric.
- Set your sewing machine to the correct stitch, length and tension and do a test run on your chosen fabric, see page 8.
- Seam allowances are included and should be stitched and trimmed back to ⅛in, see page 8.
- Before painting the doll, test the paint on a spare piece of fabric.

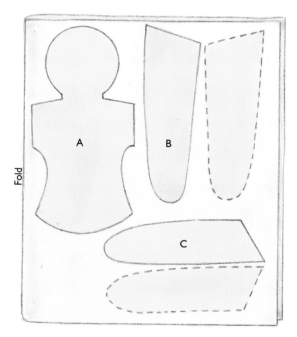

Cutting layout for muslin

THE DOLL ~ HEAD AND BODY

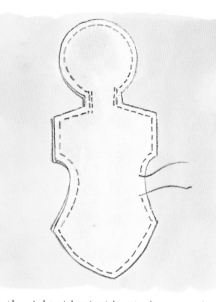

1 With the right sides inside, pin, baste, and machine stitch the two head and body pieces together, leaving a 1in opening along one side. Double stitch at each side of the neck for extra strength. Remove basting.

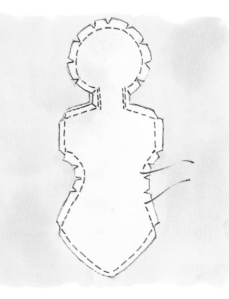

2 Using small scissors, clip the curved seam allowances just short of the stitching, at the neck, and around the head and the waist.

3 Turn right side out. Stuff and, using the end of a knitting needle to push the stuffing into the corners, make a smooth, well-padded shape. Turn in the raw edges of the opening and, using matching sewing thread, overcast to close.

ARMS AND LEGS

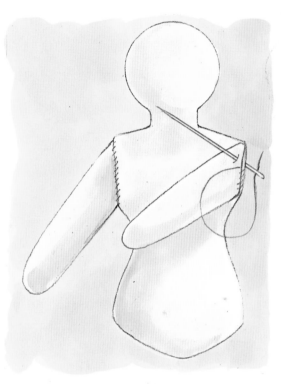

4 Machine stitch the arm pieces together in the same way, leaving the short sides open on each arm. Turn right side out and stuff evenly, as before, making sure you keep the angle as it appears on the pattern so that the arms will point down once they are stitched to the body. Using matching thread neatly slipstitch the opening to close. Attach the arms (as shown on the pattern) to the body with small overcasting stitches. Check they are all the same length.

5 Repeat in exactly the same way for the legs. You will notice that the legs are similarly angled so they will hang down neatly from the body.

HAND PAINTING THE BODY AND FACE

6 Following the color diagram given on the pattern, begin by marking the basic areas of the undergarments onto the doll with a very light pencil line. Finer details such as bows, dots, and buttons can be applied to the basic colors when they have dried. Using a fairly small brush and adding a little water to the paint, apply the appropriate colors to the panties and camisole, hands, and shoes. Leave the paint to dry thoroughly before adding the finer details such as the lace edgings, buttons, and bows. For this, use a very small brush and not too much water; otherwise, the paints may run into each other.

7 Using a light pencil line, draw the hairline, eyes, eyebrows, lips, cheeks, and necklace, freehand. Paint the eyes first, then a line around them to form the shape of the eyes and the eyebrows. Add two dots for the nose and, finally, paint the lips. To achieve the look of delicate eye make-up, water down the paint considerably and apply it carefully to the eyelids. Do the same for the cheeks. Now color in the hair and, with a steady hand, add little curls around the face. Finish by adding the necklace of multicolored beads.

The painted-on undergarments continue on the back of the doll.

CLOTHING PATTERN PIECES

• Patterns for this project are full size and do not need to be enlarged. Before pinning on the pattern pieces, see the Checklist on page 27.

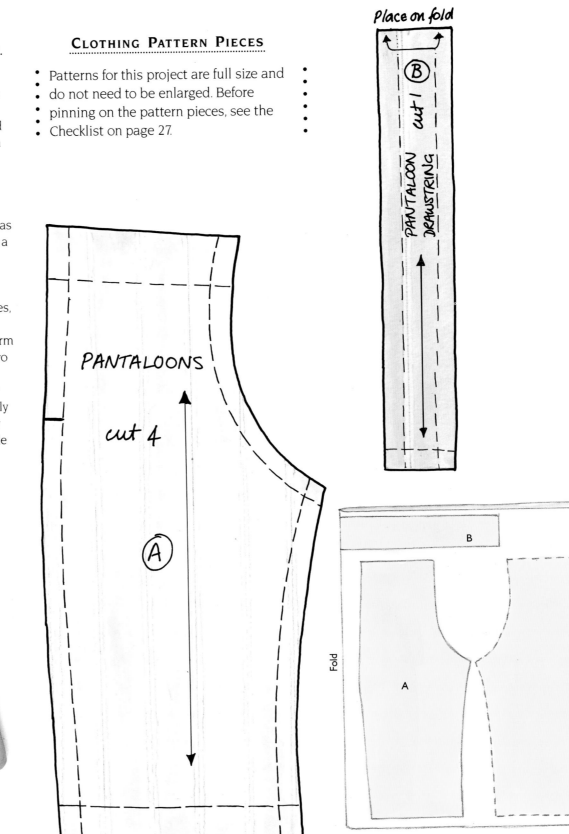

PANTALOONS

cut 4

Ⓐ

Place on fold

Ⓑ

PANTALOON DRAWSTRING cut 1

Cutting layout for fine, white cotton fabric

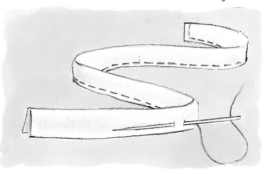

THE CLOTHES ~ PANTALOONS

1 Place the four pieces together to make two pairs and, with the right sides inside, pin, baste, and machine stitch along the curved edges of each pair.

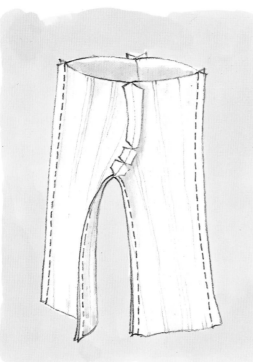

2 Clip the curved seam and press open. Place the two sections right sides together. Baste and machine stitch the inner leg seams in one continuous operation. Machine stitch the side seams and finger-press the seams open. Remove the basting stitches.

3 Make narrow double hems on each leg to finish and, using matching sewing thread, secure with a row of small running stitches. Repeat on the waist edge, but make the hem slightly bigger to allow the drawstring to be threaded through.

4 Pin the lace trim around the lower edge of each leg and, using matching sewing thread, secure with small running stitches. Overlap the lace edges on the inside leg seam for neatness.

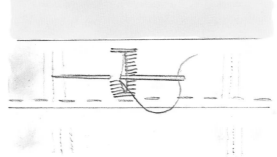

5 Turn the pantaloons right side out and, using small scissors, make an upright slit in single fabric layer at the side of the waistband, just big enough for the drawstring to pass through. Finish the edges of the slit with small buttonhole stitches, working in the same way as for a buttonhole.

6 To make the drawstring, turn under the short ends by ¼in and press. Now turn in the long sides until they meet in the middle of the fabric. Fold the fabric lengthwise, press and baste to secure. Using matching thread, hand stitch with small running stitches.

7 Attach the short end of the drawstring to a small safety pin and thread it through the waistband, ready to tie into a bow.

COSTUME DOLLS

The body of this doll has been specially designed for display and is very quick to make. So once you have followed the simple instructions for making the body, you are free to create any number of different dolls.

In particular, this technique is ideal for making a collection of dolls wearing national or traditional costumes. Start by copying the dolls here, and then research pictures of other costumes to create your own designs.

Traditional print fabrics with a strong pattern for the dress

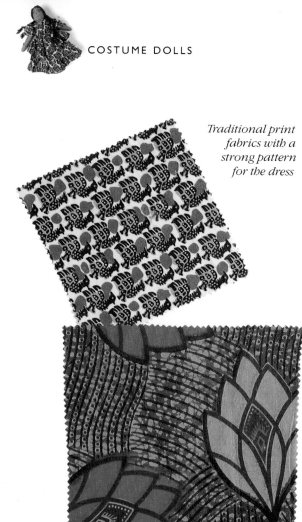

MATERIALS

DOLL (measures 9½in high)

- 12in × 18in of brown lightweight cotton fabric for the doll
- One small ball of brown or black yarn for the hair
- One cardboard tube about 4½in high for the doll base
- 4in square of cardboard, (a cereal box is suitable)
- Tape
- Synthetic stuffing or kapok
- Brown, white and red embroidery thread for the facial features
- Small beads for the jewelry
- Dried beans or pebbles for weighting the base of the doll
- White dressmaker's carbon paper

DRESS

- Two pieces of African-style print fabric measuring 12in x 28in and 10in × 20in

Small beads for the jewelry

Embroidery threads for the facial features

Thread small shells to make a necklace

Alternative fabrics could be chosen

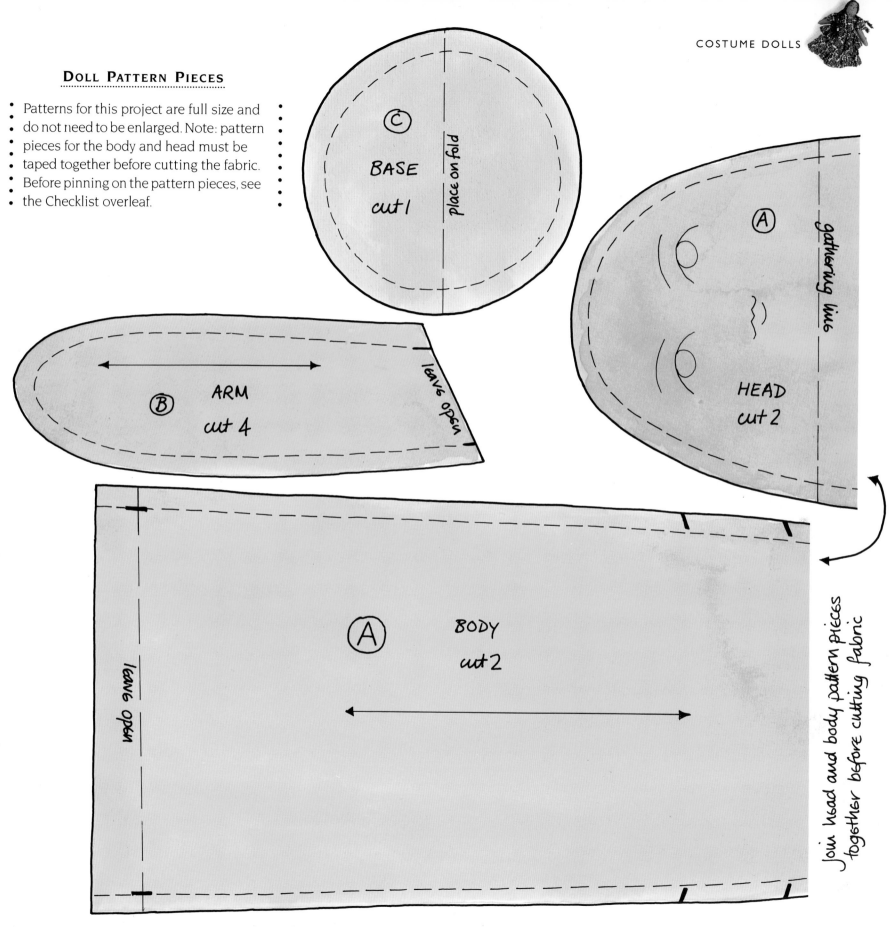

DOLL PATTERN PIECES

- Patterns for this project are full size and do not need to be enlarged. Note: pattern pieces for the body and head must be taped together before cutting the fabric. Before pinning on the pattern pieces, see the Checklist overleaf.

Ⓒ BASE cut 1 — place on fold

Ⓐ HEAD cut 2 — gathering line

Ⓑ ARM cut 4 — leave open

Ⓐ BODY cut 2 — leave open

Join head and body pattern pieces together before cutting fabric

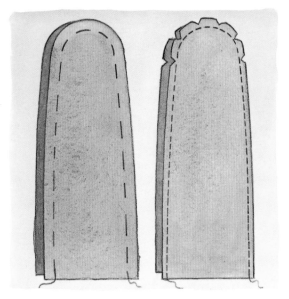

The cardboard tube is filled with dried beans to stabilize it.

2 Fill the tube with dried beans, for example, or small pebbles until it feels fairly sturdy. Then place the other cardboard circle on top and attach it as before. Put the tube to one side.

3 With right sides together, place the two head and body pieces together. Pin, baste, and machine stitch around, leaving the bottom edge open.

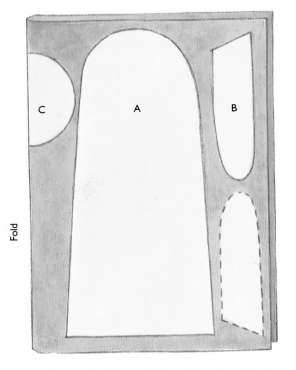

Cutting layout for brown lightweight cotton fabric

C   A   B

Fold

THE DOLL ~ BODY AND HEAD

1 Place the cardboard tube on the piece of cardboard and draw around its base. Draw a second circle and cut out both pieces. Using tape, attach one circular piece to one end of the tube.

4 Trim the seam to ⅛in and, using sharp scissors, cut small notches into the curved seam allowance just short of the stitching. Now turn right side out

34

and lightly press. Before stuffing the head, trace the facial details shown on the pattern piece and, using dressmaker's carbon paper, transfer them to the doll.

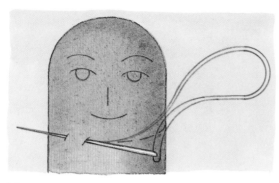

5 Use double sewing thread knotted at one end to run a line of gathering stitches all the way around to form the neck, as shown on the pattern piece. Leave a length of sewing thread so that you can rethread it later and pull up the stitches to form the head.

6 With well-teased-out stuffing, fill the head above the line of stitching until it is quite firm. It may help to use the end of a knitting needle to push the stuffing in firmly. Once you have filled the head, rethread your needle with the sewing thread left earlier. Pull the thread firmly so that the fabric is tightly gathered. This forms the neck. Secure with a couple of oversewn stitches.

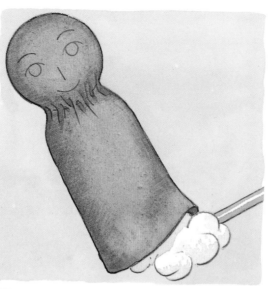

7 Continue to stuff the body to a depth of approximately 3in using a knitting needle to help give it a fairly firm finish. This forms the middle of the body. Run a row of gathering stitches along the bottom edge about ⅜in in, and leave the thread ungathered.

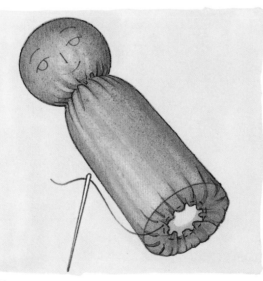

8 Ease the cardboard tube into the bottom half of the body. Check that there is the right amount of stuffing to form the middle of the body. Then pull the gathering thread tight and overcast to secure so that the tube is held in place. The whole shape should be quite firm, sturdy and straight.

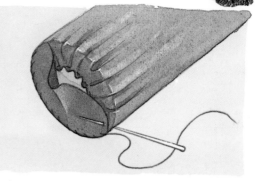

9 Clip into the curved seam allowance of the doll base. Turn the seam under and press flat. Pin it to the base of the doll to finish. With matching thread, neatly overcast around the edge.

ARMS

10 With right sides inside, place the four arm pieces together to make two arms. Baste and machine stitch around each arm piece, leaving the short straight sides open ready for turning right side out. Trim the seams, and clip the curved seam allowance of each arm. Turn them both right side out and stuff, using the end of a knitting needle to reach into the "hand".

HAIR

13 From the ball of wool, cut 72 lengths about 5in long (depending on how long you want to make the hair). Divide the wool into twelve sets of six strands and secure each set with a knot at one end.

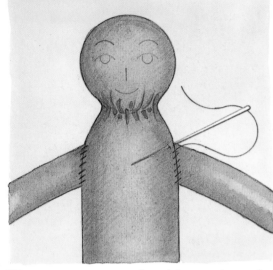

11 Turn under the raw edge of the opening and slipstitch to close. Matching the arms to the positioning marks given on the pattern, attach them to the doll using small overcasting stitches.

FACE

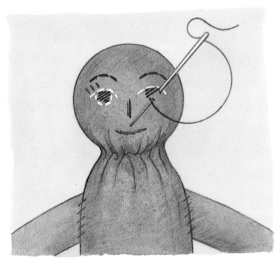

12 Using the appropriate colors (two strands in the needle if using stranded floss), embroider the facial details. With the brown thread, work the doll's eyebrows in stem stitch and her eyes in satin stitch. Using white thread outline her eyes and eyelids with backstitches, suggesting eyelashes with four diagonal straight stitches. Continuing with white thread, work the nose in stem stitch. Finish by embroidering the mouth in red with two rows of stem stitch.

14 Using matching thread, attach the hair to the head with backstitching. The knots should lie on the seamline on top of the head, with the wool strands falling over the face. Continue to attach all twelve hair pieces in the same way around the edge of the face.

15 Plait each hair piece and secure the ends by tying them around with a length of thread. Then slip stitch each plait to the back of the head, passing the needle through the thickness of the plait, until you reach the back of the neck. The plaits should lie neatly side-by-side, covering the back of the head.

JEWELRY

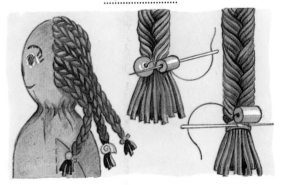

16 Decorate the hair by attaching small beads, sequins, or tiny shells to each braid, stitching groups of two, three, or four mixed colors at the point where the braid was secured with matching thread. Similarly, thread enough tiny beads to make a bracelet and necklace. In each case, attach them with one or two overcasting stitches to the back of the wrist and at the back of the neck respectively. Make the necklace long enough to fit just inside the "V"neck of the dress.

CLOTHING PATTERN PIECES

Patterns for this project are full size and do not need to be enlarged. Before pinning on the pattern pieces, see the Checklist on page 34.

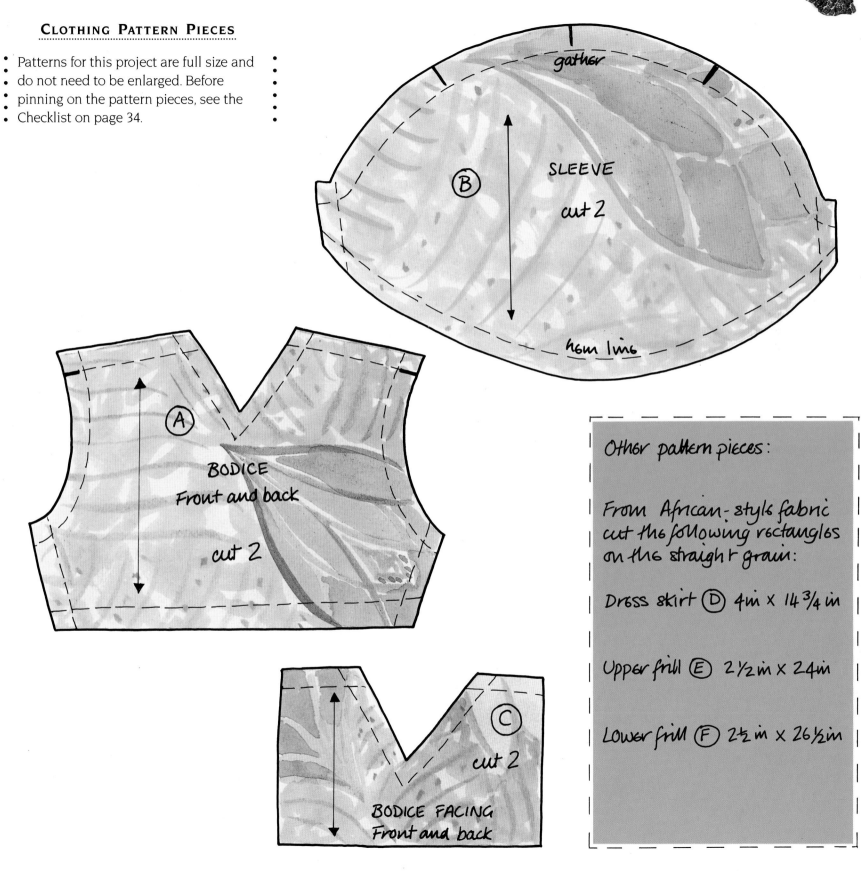

gather

(B) SLEEVE
cut 2

hem line

(A) BODICE
Front and back

cut 2

(C) cut 2

BODICE FACING
Front and back

Other pattern pieces:

From African-style fabric cut the following rectangles on the straight grain:

Dress skirt (D) 4in × 14¾in

Upper frill (E) 2½in × 24in

Lower frill (F) 2½in × 26½in

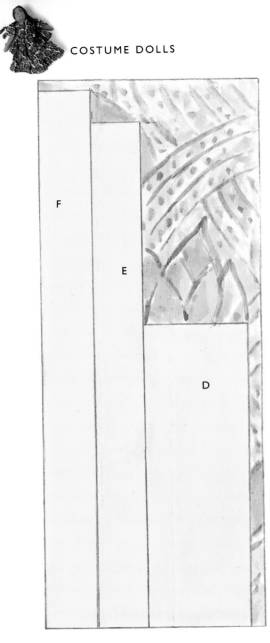

Cutting layout for African-style fabric: single layer

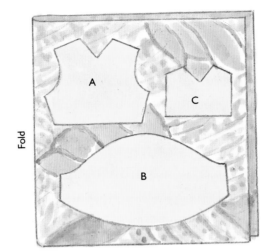

Cutting layout for African-style fabric: folded

3 With the right sides inside, pin, baste, and stitch the two bodice pieces together at the shoulder seams and side seams. Press open.

THE CLOTHES ~
DRESS

1 With the right sides inside, place one section of the bodice facing and one of the bodice pieces together, lining up the "V"neck. Pin, baste, and then machine stitch around the "V"neck. Repeat on the second bodice piece.

2 Clip the seam allowance, just short of the stitching and turn the facing on both bodice pieces to the wrong side, leaving a neat seam along the neckline. Press.

4 With each sleeve, place the underarm seams together, right sides inside, then baste and machine stitch. Press the seams open. Make a line of running stitches along the sleeve cap just inside the seam allowance. Gather gently so that the sleeve fits the armhole.

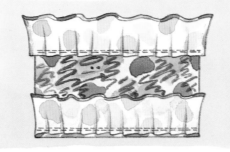

7 Attach the lower ruffle in the same way as for the upper ruffle but, this time, align the edge of the ruffle with the edges of the main skirt. Remove all basting threads.

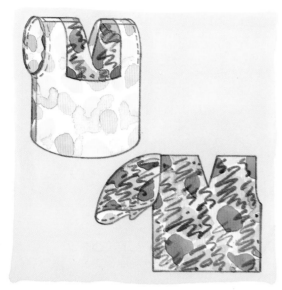

5 Insert the sleeve into the armhole, right sides together and, with shoulder seam and balance points matching, pin, baste and either machine stitch or hand sew in place using small back-stitches. Make a small hem on the lower edge of the sleeve, baste, and slipstitch.

6 On each ruffle, begin by machine stitching a narrow double hem along one long edge. For the upper ruffle, pleat the raw edge with ¼in wide pleats spaced about 1in apart. Pin, baste, and machine stitch to hold. With right sides together, place the pleated ruffle, as shown in the diagram, about 1in from the waist edge of the main skirt. Make sure the short edges of the ruffle overlap the main skirt by ¼in. Pin, baste, and machine stitch in place.

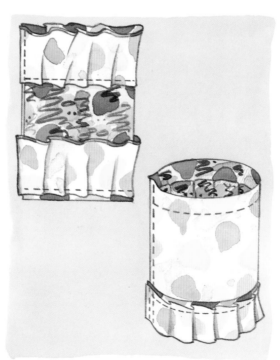

8 With right sides inside, place the two short edges of the upper ruffle together and machine stitch. With the skirt right sides together, baste, and machine stitch along the skirt and the lower ruffle in one continuous seam. Stitch above the top ruffle. Lightly press the ruffles so that they lie correctly.

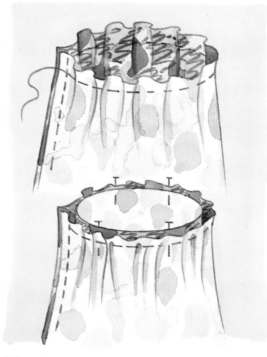

9 Gather the top of the skirt on a line just inside the seam allowance, and pull up the thread so that the skirt waist fits the bodice. With right sides inside, pin, baste, and machine stitch the skirt and bodice together. Finish the seams and turn right side out.

HEADSCARF

10 As an alternative to the braids, you may wish to make a headscarf for your doll from a square of leftover fabric and simply knot it in front or behind her head.

ASLEEP OR AWAKE? THE SURPRISING UPSIDEDOWN DOLL CHANGES HER

EXPRESSION TO BE BOTH A DAYTIME TOY AND THE IDEAL DOLL FOR

CHILDREN TO CUDDLE AT NIGHT.

UPSIDEDOWN DOLL

Bold, bright colors for daytime wear and more subdued patterns for her night attire make the intriguing upsidedown doll a beautiful toy whichever way up she is!

The doll has two heads – one with a wide-awake daytime expression and the other with the eyes closed for the night. Two skirts, joined at the waist, give the doll two different outfits and can be pulled up or down to reveal the appropriate face.

The daytime doll has her hair in bunches, while the nighttime doll has a little matching cap. Take care with the embroidered faces and you will create a toy to treasure.

MATERIALS

DOLL (measures 20in high)

- 18in of 36in-wide lightweight muslin for the body
- Synthetic stuffing or kapok
- 2oz of bulky knitting yarn for the hair
- 1yd of ⅝in-wide ribbon for the hair
- 27in of 59in-wide cotton fabric for the day dress
- 27in of 59in-wide contrasting cotton fabric for the nightgown and nightcap
- 12in square of cotton fabric for the nightcap lining
- 18in of 1in-wide lace trim for the day dress
- 18in of 1½in-wide lace trim for the nightgown neck
- 1½yds of ¾in-wide gathered lace trim for the nightgown sleeves and nightcap
- 1yd of ⅛in-wide ribbon to trim the nightgown
- 2yds of ½in-wide ribbon for both dress belts
- Stranded embroidery floss in black, red, and blue for the facial details
- Shirring elastic
- Fabric glue

DOLL PATTERN PIECES

Patterns for this project should be enlarged to twice the size. If you have access to a photocopier with an enlarging facility set it to 200%. Otherwise trace off the patterns on to a grid, following the procedure outlined on page 7. (See also the Checklist on the opposite page).

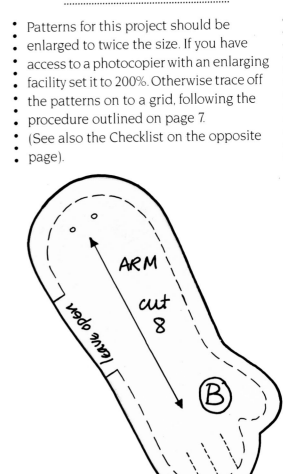

Neck trim

Muslin for the body

Contrasting cotton fabric for the day and night dress

Heavy yarn for the hair

Cutting layout for muslin

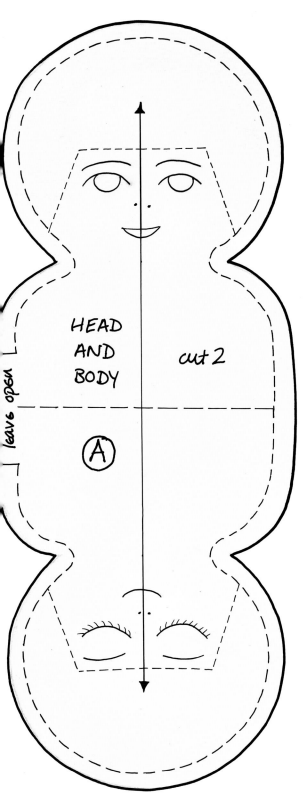

HEAD AND BODY   cut 2

(A)

leave open

THE DOLL ~ BODY

Note: before stitching the body section together, you will find it helpful to trace the facial details and transfer them to the muslin using dressmaker's carbon paper.

1 With the two muslin pieces right sides together, machine stitch around the body leaving an opening down one side, as indicated on the pattern. Clip the curved seam allowances and turn right side out. Press. Insert the filling using a knitting needle to push the stuffing in evenly. Overcast the edges of the opening to close.

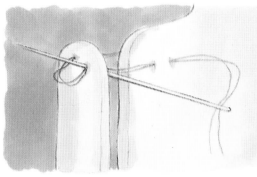

2 Make two pairs of arms in the same way and then sew them to the body, aligning them with the points as marked on the pattern. With a doubled

thread in the needle, make three or four stitches, as shown in the diagram, stitching through the same places in the body and arm for neatness and for added strength.

3 Wrap the sewing thread around the stitches between the body and arms to form a shank so that the arms can swing freely. Take the wrapping thread back through the arm and secure within the holding threads.

4 Outline the fingers with backstitch along the lines shown. Using matching thread, make sure the beginning and ending of the stitching is secure. Pull the stitching firmly to give form to the fingers.

SLEEPING DOLL'S HAIR

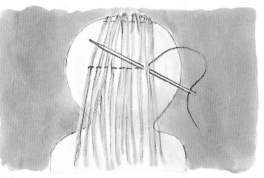

5 To make bangs, cut about 20 lengths of yarn 12in long and anchor the ends of the yarn to the top of the head with one or two backstitches, allowing the yarn to fall forward over the face. Backstitch the strands to the head along the bangs line and then fold them back again where they can be stitched in place to the top of the head and also along the neckline.

6 Cut enough 9in lengths of yarn to make a hank which, when tied in the middle and placed on top of the head, will fully cover the area from the hairline on the face to the back of the head covering the yarn previously brought over from the bangs. Glue or backstitch onto the head.

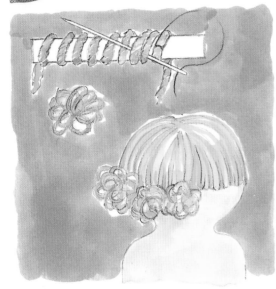

7 For the remaining hair, wind lengths of yarn around a ruler and secure each loop with a line of backstitch. Slip the loops off the ruler and backstitch or glue them in place along the neckline covering the existing ends of yarn. Repeat as necessary until the neckline is covered.

WAKING DOLL'S HAIR

8 Make the bangs in the same way as for the sleeping doll (see step 5). For the remaining hair, cut enough 16in lengths of yarn to make a hank which, when tied in the middle and placed on top (center) of the head, will cover the area from the hairline on the face to the back of the head. Separate the yarn to each side and then glue or backstitch into place along the back neckline. Tie bunches at each side with ribbon bows and trim the ends if necessary.

FACES

9 Using the appropriate colors, embroider the features as shown on the pattern. Work the eyebrows and eye outlines in stem stitch, using three strands of black thread. Fill in the mouth with stem stitch using three strands of red thread. Work the pupils in satin stitch using three strands of black, and the irises in buttonhole stitch with three strands of blue. Suggest the nose with two French knots using two strands of black thread.

CLOTHING PATTERN PIECES

Patterns for this project should be enlarged to twice the size. If you have access to a photocopier with an enlarging facility, set it to 200%. Otherwise, trace the patterns on a grid, following the procedure outlined on page 7. (See also the Checklist on page 43).

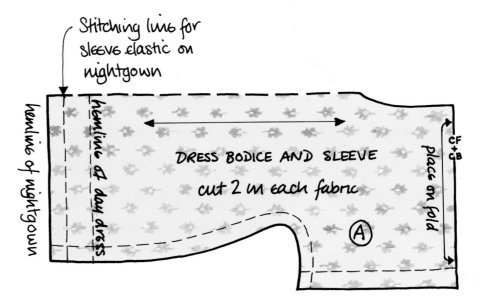

Stitching line for sleeves elastic on nightgown

hemline of nightgown

hemline of nightgown

hemline of day dress

DRESS BODICE AND SLEEVE

cut 2 in each fabric

place on fold

CF + CB

Ⓐ

Other pattern pieces:

For the mob cap Ⓑ cut out one circle 11 in. in diameter from the nightgown fabric, and a second circle from plain fabric for the lining.

For the dress skirts Ⓒ cut two rectangles, each 13 in. x 36 in., one from daydress fabric, and one from nightgown fabric.

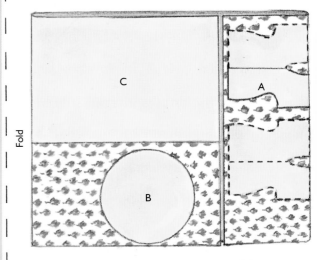

Cutting layout for white patterned fabric and yellow patterned fabric

THE CLOTHES ~ SKIRT

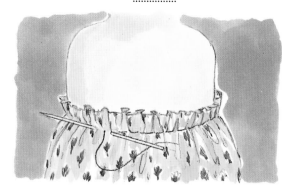

1 With the right sides facing, machine stitch each skirt piece separately along the short edge, and press the seams open. Pin and machine stitch both pieces together, right sides inside, along the hem edge, then turn right side out and press. Using a long machine stitch, make a line of gathering stitches around each waistline. Pull up the gathers until each skirt waist fits around the waistline of the doll. Pin and backstitch to secure.

NIGHTGOWN BODICE

2 Make a single hem on each sleeve edge and cover with eyelet lace trim. Machine stitch. Using elastic thread on the machine spool and a long machine stitch, sew ½in in from the hem to form the elasticized cuff. With the right sides facing, machine stitch the back and front bodice pieces together along the sleeve and side seam.

3 With the right side outside, fit the bodice on the doll. Turn under the seam allowance at the waistline and hemstitch in place. Turn in the seam allowance at the neck and overcast for about 1in along each shoulder line.

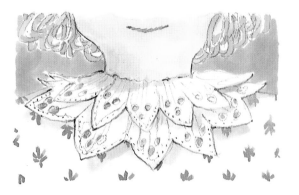

4 Gather the 1½in-wide lace to fit around the neck. Turn under one raw edge and overlap to finish, then hemstitch by hand. Tie the narrow ribbon around the wrists in bows and finish with a third bow stitched to the center front neck. Tie 1yd of the ½in-wide ribbon around the waist.

NIGHTCAP

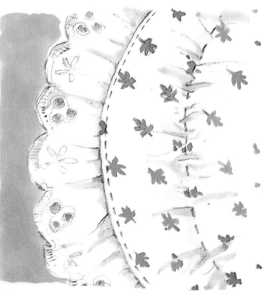

5 With right sides facing, machine stitch around the edge taking a ¼in seam allowance and leaving a 2in opening for turning right side out. Clip the seam allowance, turn right side out, and slipstitch the opening to close. Press. Pin and machine stitch the eyelet lace trim to the edge. Using elastic thread make a line of gathering stitches 1in from the edge of the circle as for the nightgown sleeves.

DAY DRESS BODICE

6 Make a line of running stitches as shown on the sleeve hem and trim to within ¼in of the stitching. With the right sides facing, machine stitch the back and front bodice sections together along the sleeve and side seam in a continuous line. Continue as for step 3.

7 Cut the required lengths of 1in-wide trim to fit around the hem of the sleeves and the neck of the dress. Turn under the raw edge, pin in place, and with matching thread, hemstitch to secure. Tie 1yd of ½in-wide ribbon around the waist and finish in a bow.

AMISH-STYLE DOLLS

Traditional Amish dolls are not given faces, in keeping with the biblical commandment forbidding graven images. Usually dressed in plain greens, blues and purples, we have chosen more upbeat checks and stripes for our dolls.

There are only two pieces – the effect of separate arms and legs is given by easing the stuffing away from the joints and sewing across them. Using fabric paint for the hair and shoes helps keep the overall effect simple, and in keeping with the Amish origins.

47

MATERIALS

DOLLS (measure 11½in high)

- 8in × 14in of lightweight, muslin for each doll
- Synthetic stuffing or kapok
- Black fabric paint for the boy's shoes and hair
- Brown fabric paint for the girl's hair
- Deep blue fabric paint for the girl's shoes
- Small paintbrush

BOY'S CLOTHES

- 10in × 11½in of lightweight, striped cotton for the shirt
- 6½in × 15in of lightweight denim for the overalls
- 5in square of black felt for the hat

GIRL'S CLOTHES

- 9½in × 14in of blue and white striped cotton fabric for the blouse
- 9in × 20in of a small-check gingham fabric for the skirt
- 6½in × 9in of fine lightweight cotton fabric for the apron
- 5in × 6in of plain white cotton fabric for the bonnet
- 8in of ⅜in-wide lace trim for the bonnet ties
- Sprigs of lavender for the pocket

Denim and striped cotton for the boy's clothes

Light cotton for the apron and bonnet

Blue and white striped cotton and red checks for the girl's clothes

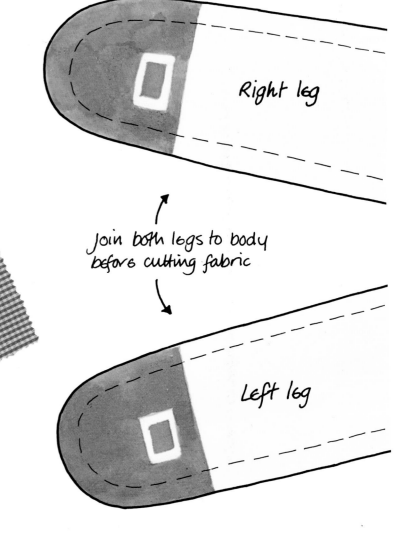

Right leg

Join both legs to body before cutting fabric

Left leg

*Muslin for the
dolls' bodies*

DOLL PATTERN PIECES

Patterns for this project are full size and do not need to be enlarged. Note: left and right leg pieces must be joined to the body piece before cutting the fabric. Before pinning on the pattern pieces, see the Checklist on page 50. Details for the girl doll are shown overleaf.

join right leg

join left leg

HEAD AND BODY

cut 2

leave open

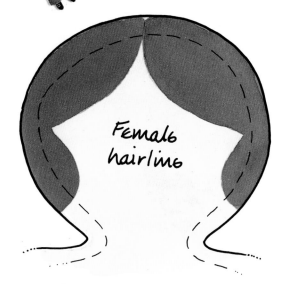

For the girl doll, trace off the shoe and hairline details and transfer them to the boy's body.

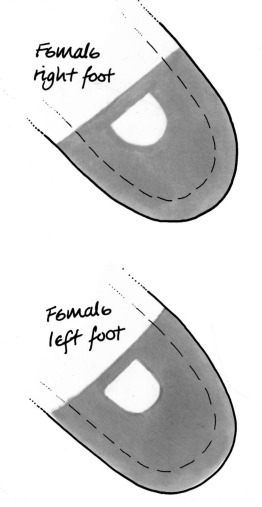

THE DOLL ~
BODY AND HEAD

1 Pin the two body pieces together, right sides facing, and machine stitch around the edge taking a ¼in seam and leaving an opening along one side, as shown on the pattern.

2 On a doll like this with fixed arms and legs and of a size that demands narrow seams, it is a good idea to double-sew around the underarms, the neck, and between the legs for extra strength.

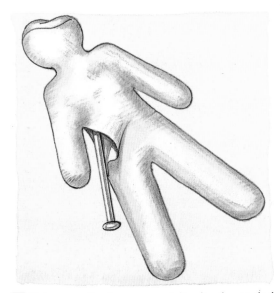

3 Using small scissors, carefully clip the angled seams as shown on the pattern, and around the curved seams, being careful not to snip into the stitches. Turn the doll to the right side, carefully pushing out the limbs and head with the help of a knitting needle. Press.

4 Using well-teased-out stuffing, begin to stuff the doll starting with the head. Then stuff the arms and the legs and the body last of all. Use the end of a knitting needle to get the stuffing right into the corners evenly and firmly.

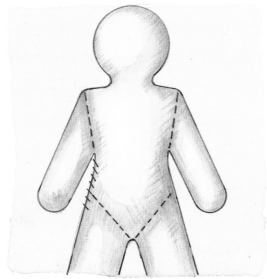

CLOTHING PATTERN PIECES
FOR BOY

Patterns for this project are full size and do not need to be enlarged. The shirt pieces are shown overleaf. Before pinning on the pattern pieces, see the Checklist opposite.

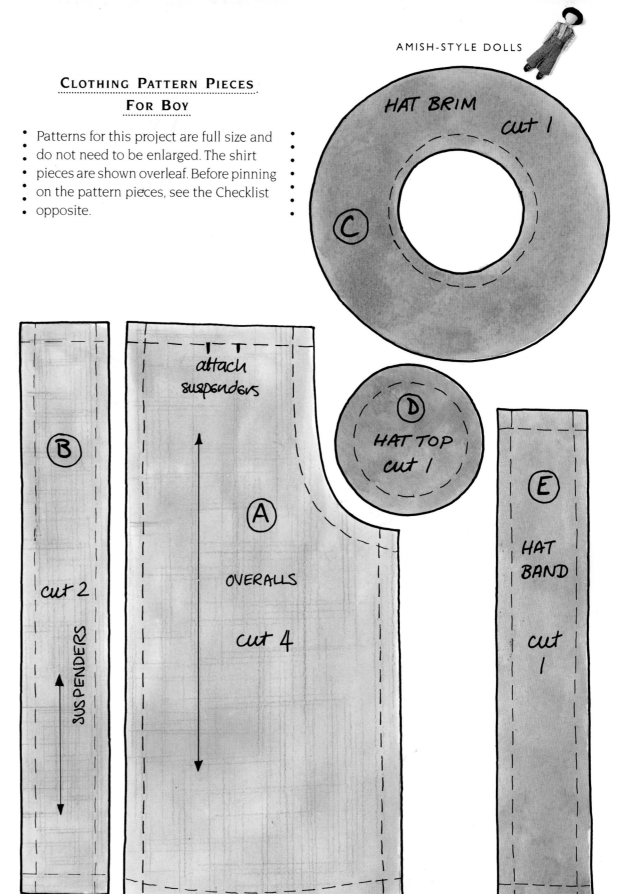

HAT BRIM
cut 1
C

D
HAT TOP
cut 1

E
HAT BAND
cut 1

B
cut 2
SUSPENDERS

attach suspenders
A
OVERALLS
cut 4

5 Turn in the raw edges of the opening and, with a doubled thread in the needle, neatly overcast to close. Sew a line of stitches along the tops of the legs and arms, stitching through all layers. This will allow the doll's limbs to bend slightly.

6 Working freehand with a light pencil, draw the appropriate male or female shape of the shoes and the hairline onto the doll. Color them in with the fabric paint (following the manufacturer's instructions) and leave to dry.

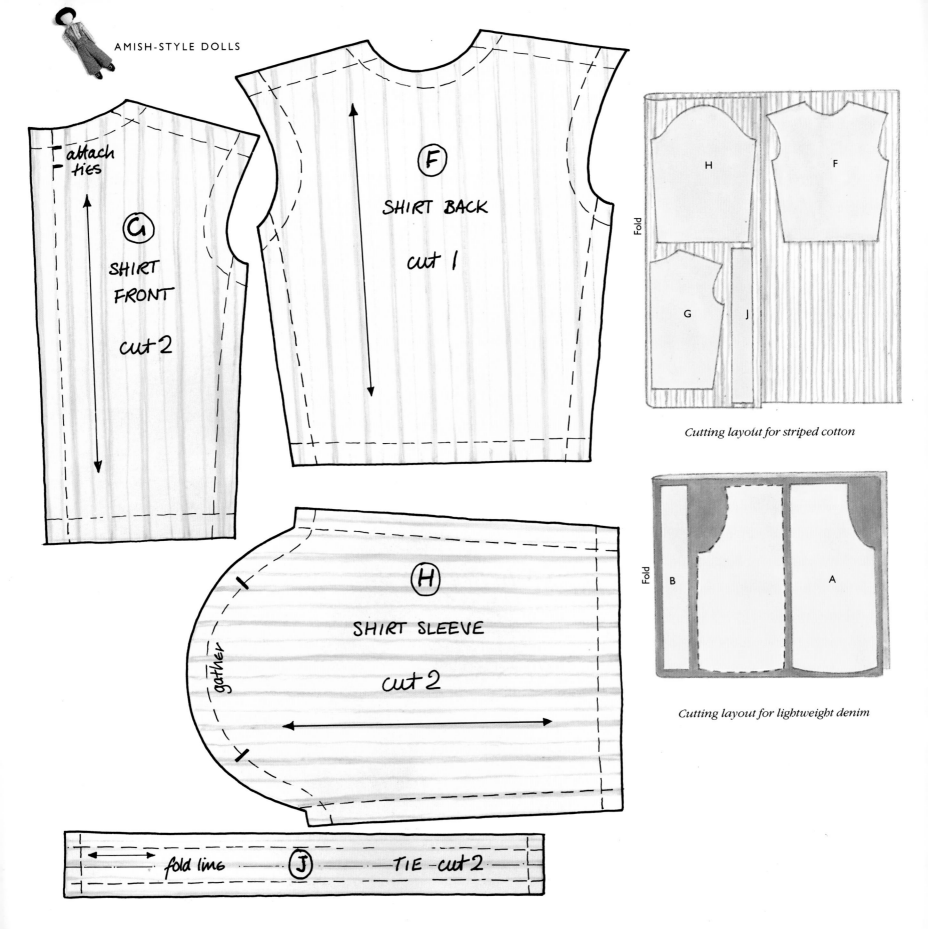

attach
ties

Ⓖ

SHIRT
FRONT

cut 2

Ⓕ

SHIRT BACK

cut 1

Ⓗ

SHIRT SLEEVE

cut 2

gather

Ⓙ   fold line   TIE · cut 2

H

F

G   J

Fold

Cutting layout for striped cotton

B   A

Fold

Cutting layout for lightweight denim

BOY'S CLOTHES ~ SHIRT

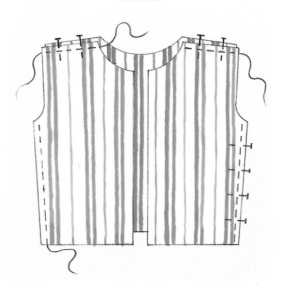

1 With the right sides facing, pin the two shirt fronts to the back shirt piece. Machine stitch taking ¼in seams. Press the seams open.

2 In the same way, stitch the sleeve seams together and press them open. Lightly gather the sleeve cap and pin the sleeves into the armholes, gently easing the fullness to the top of the sleeve. Hand stitch the sleeve in place with small backstitches.

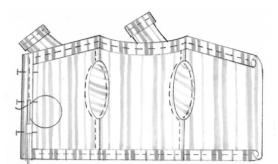

3 Making the tiniest double hems, finish the raw edges by hand at the sleeve wrists, along the neckline, around the bottom edge and down the front edges using matching thread and neat running stitches. Press on the wrong side.

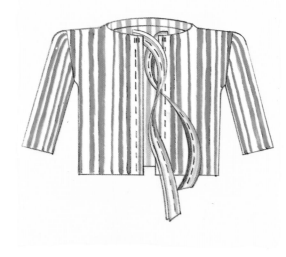

4 To make the ties for the shirt, fold in the two long edges so that they meet in the middle and then fold in half. Stitch along the length with running stitches, turn under each end, and secure with one or two overcasting stitches. Attach the ties to the neck edge of the shirt front with overcasting stitches.

OVERALLS

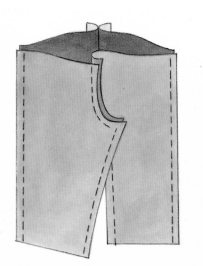

5 Place the four pants leg pieces together to make two pairs. With the right sides facing, pin and machine stitch around the crotch seam. Clip the curved seam allowance and press open. Open the two leg pieces and, with right sides together, pin

and machine stitch around the inside leg seams in one continuous movement. Stitch the two outside leg seams and press all seams open.

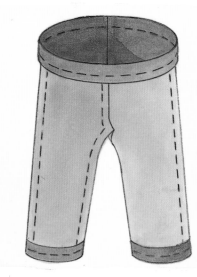

6 To finish the raw edges along the top and bottoms of the pants, make narrow double hems and secure with running stitch.

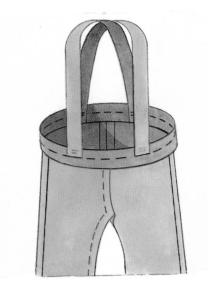

7 Make suspenders in a similar way to the shirt ties, stitching along the length with a row of running stitches. Attach the suspenders to the front and back of the overalls on the inside waist edge, neatly overcasting to secure. Cross the suspenders at the back to give an authentic touch.

HAT

Note: as felt is a bonded fabric, care should be taken when handling, especially with some lightweight varieties. Do not, for example, pull knots through as they may tear the felt with disastrous results.

8 Pin the two short sides of the hat band together and, using tiny running stitches, join to form a circle.

9 Fit the top piece into the circular band and join the two edges together. Working with the top uppermost, stitch through both thicknesses pulling the thread fairly firmly to give the finished seam a good shape.

10 In the same way, attach the hat brim to the hat working with the brim uppermost. Trim the seams, if necessary, and turn right side out.

CLOTHING PATTERN PIECES
FOR GIRL

- Patterns for this project are full size and do not need to be enlarged. Before pinning on the pattern pieces, see the Checklist on page 50.

Ⓛ BONNET BACK cut 1 gather

Ⓜ BONNET NECK FACING cut 1

Ⓚ BONNET FRONT cut 1 pleats pleats

gather

Ⓒ BLOUSE SLEEVE cut 2

Ⓑ BLOUSE BACK cut 2

fold here Ⓓ BLOUSE TIE cut 2

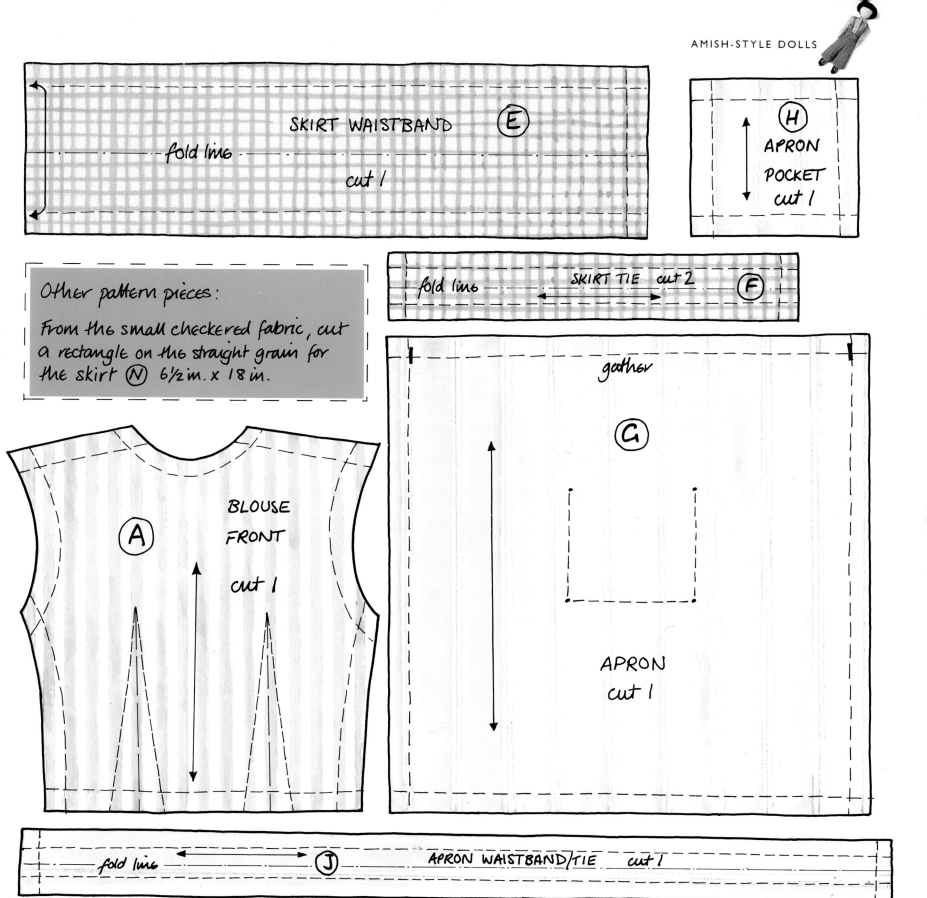

SKIRT WAISTBAND (E)

fold line

cut 1

(H) APRON POCKET cut 1

Other pattern pieces:

From the small checkered fabric, cut a rectangle on the straight grain for the skirt (N) 6½ in. x 18 in.

fold line   SKIRT TIE   cut 2   (F)

gather

(G)

APRON cut 1

(A) BLOUSE FRONT cut 1

fold line   (J)   APRON WAISTBAND/TIE   cut 1

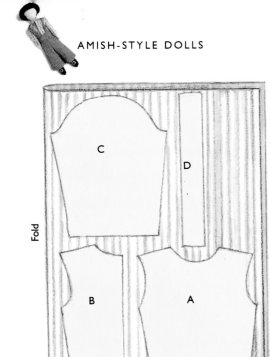

Cutting layout for blue and white striped cotton

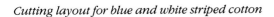

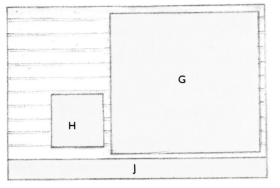

Cutting layout for white cotton fabric

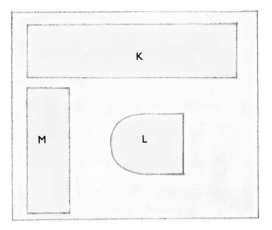

Cutting layout for cotton fabric

GIRL'S CLOTHES ~ SKIRT

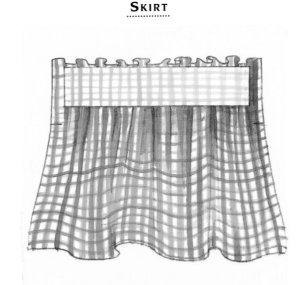

1 Make a line of gathering stitches along the top edge of the skirt, just inside the seam allowance. Pull up the thread until the waist edge is longer than the waistband by ⅜in.

2 With the right sides facing, pin the two short sides of the skirt together and machine stitch to within 1½in of the waist edge. Press open. Finish the opening by hemming a narrow double hem on both sides.

3 Pin the waistband to the gathered edge of the skirt, with the right sides together and the seam

allowances extending on each side. Machine stitch in place taking a ⅜in seam. Turn in the two short edges of the waistband and press the fold.

4 Fold the waistband over to the wrong side, turn under the raw edge, and hand stitch to secure.

5 To make the ties for the skirt, first press a single hem on the two short edges, then fold the two long edges in so that they meet in the middle. Fold in half and then hand stitch along the length of the tie using tiny running stitches. Make the second tie and overcast in place to each side of the opening on the inside of the waistband.

BLOUSE

6 Begin by making the two darts on the blouse front. Pin and either machine stitch or backstitch to secure. Press the darts toward the center front.

7 With the right sides facing, pin the two blouse back sections to the blouse front piece. Machine stitch the two side seams and shoulder seams and press them open.

8 Make a line of running stitches around the sleeve cap and lightly gather to fit the armhole. With right sides facing, stitch the sleeve seams together. Pin the sleeves into the armhole also with the right sides facing. Even out the gathers and line up the underarm seam with the side seam of the blouse. Backstitch in place.

9 Making the tiniest double hems, finish the bottom of the sleeves, around the neck, the back opening, and around the bottom edge of the blouse using small running stitches.

10 Make the ties as for the boy's shirt. Stitch in place to each side of the back opening inside the neck edge, overcasting to secure.

APRON

11 Begin by machine stitching double hems on the two side edges of the apron, and then the bottom edge. Finish the pocket by making single hems around three sides, and stitching a double hem on the top edge. Attach the pocket to the center of the apron, as shown on the pattern, leaving the top edge open.

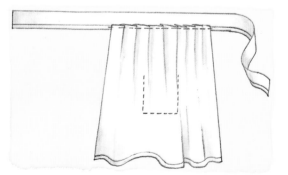

12 Pleat the top edge of the apron with ¼in deep pleats until it measures 2½in across. Pin and baste the pleats in place. With right sides together, pin the waistband/tie centrally over the apron with edges matching and stitch across.

13 Turn in the two short edges. Fold the waistband tie to the wrong side, turn under the seam allowance, and hand stitch along the entire length using small running stitches.

BONNET

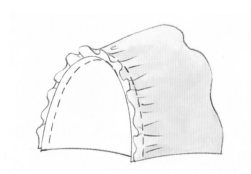

14 Make a line of running stitches along one long edge of the main bonnet piece. Pull up the thread so that the gathered edge fits around the back bonnet section. With right sides together, pin and hand stitch the two pieces together, stitching with the back section uppermost.

15 Finish the front edge of the bonnet, with the tiniest double hem secured with running stitches. Make three small pleats at each side to help shape the bonnet, and neatly overcast in place. Gather the neck edge of the bonnet until the edge is the same length as the neck facing.

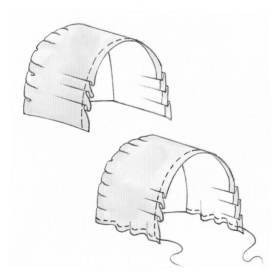

16 With right sides together, pin the neck facing to the bonnet and stitch across. Fold in the two short edges of the neck facing, make a single hem on the long edge and hand stitch to the inside of the bonnet. Overcast the ends to finish and attach the lace ties to each side.

There is something very appealing about well-worn and therefore well-loved toys. If you haven't been lucky enough to inherit any antique cloth dolls, it is very easy to create your own – either for display or as very unusual and charming gifts. These dolls hark back to the days when, if there was time to make toys, they would be made from any odd, leftover scraps. So don't spend a lot of money on fabric or hair. See what you have lying around at home. Perhaps some outgrown children's clothes can make a body, or an old dress could be used to furnish buttons for the eyes. Remember that a slightly lopsided body and big stitches are part of the charm of these dolls.

IMAGINE YOU HAVE BEEN

EXPLORING IN GREAT GRANDMA'S

ATTIC - THESE ARE JUST THE SORT

OF TOYS YOU WOULD BE

THRILLED TO FIND TUCKED

AWAY THERE.

OLD-
FASHIONED

DOLLS

MATERIALS

BOY DOLL (measures 14in high)

- 11in × 22in of narrow-wale corduroy
- Synthetic stuffing or kapok
- Two buttons about ½in across for eyes
- Embroidery thread in red for the facial details and in brown, black, beige for the hair

JEANS AND HAT

- 12in × 20in of old blue denim
- 1½in × 1½in of contrasting cotton fabric for the knee patch

SHIRT

- 10in × 15in of gingham or checked fabric
- Two old pearl buttons about ⅜in across
- Two snaps
- 1½in × 1½in of contrasting cotton fabric for the patch

BOOTS

- 6in square of black felt
- Light-colored thick embroidery thread for the laces

Fabrics for the boy doll

Old beads and buttons for adding detail

Cotton fabrics for the girl doll

A selection of lace trims

MATERIALS

GIRL DOLL (measures 12in high)

- 12in × 19in medium-weight cotton or muslin for the doll
- Synthetic stuffing or kapok
- Stranded embroidery floss in brown and blue for the hair and face, green embroidery thread for the shoes
- Fabric paints in brown, blue, and red for the face and hair
- Small paintbrush and pencil
- Cold tea
- Two old pearl buttons approx ⁵⁄₁₆in across

DRESS

- 11in × 13in of old floral cotton fabric, such as lawn
- 12in of 1in-wide old straight-edged lace for the hem
- 6in of ½in-wide old lace for the neck
- Old fabric trimming such as a silk or lace flower

PANTALOONS

- 7½in × 14in of old contrasting floral fabric
- 6in of ¾in-wide old lace

HAT

- 10in × 12in of contrasting floral fabric
- 9in of ⅜in-wide ribbon
- 12in of old ½in-wide lace trim
- Old buttons or small fabric flowers

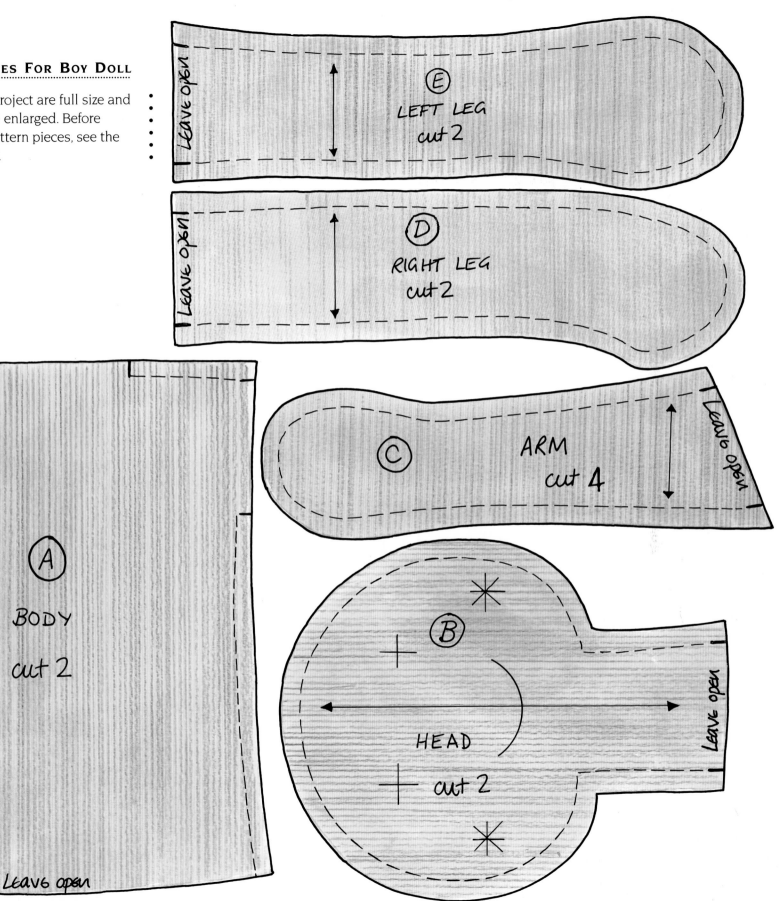

PATTERN PIECES FOR BOY DOLL

- Patterns for this project are full size and
- do not need to be enlarged. Before
- pinning on the pattern pieces, see the
- Checklist overleaf.

Leave open

E
LEFT LEG
cut 2

Leave open

D
RIGHT LEG
cut 2

A
BODY
cut 2

Leave open

C

ARM
cut 4

Leave open

B
HEAD
cut 2

Leave open

CHECKLIST

- Trace off the outline of the actual size pattern pieces, transfer all marks and cut out, see pages 6-7.
- Wash and press all fabrics to test for shrinkage. "Antique" both the doll fabric and the clothes fabric, see page 6.
- Cut out the required number for each pattern piece from the appropriate fabric.
- Set your sewing machine to the correct stitch, length and tension and do a test run on your chosen fabric, see page 8.
- Seam allowances are included and should be stitched and trimmed back to ⅛in, see page 8.

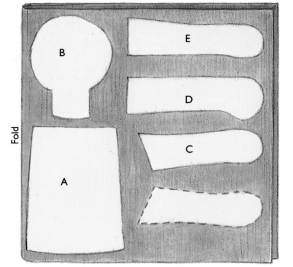

Cutting layout for narrow-wall corduroy

BOY DOLL ~ HEAD AND ARMS

Note: in order to give the boy old-fashioned doll an authentic homemade look, it would be better to hand stitch the doll throughout, taking particular notice of the uneven legs and oddly shaped feet and hands, and so on.

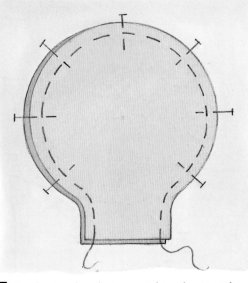

1 Pin the two head pieces right sides together and backstitch around them, leaving the neck open. Clip the neck angle and around the curved seam before turning right side out. Stuff evenly to give a smooth shape. Pin the neck edges together and put to one side.

2 Backstitch the arm pieces together, clip the curved seams, turn, and stuff in a similar way. Use the end of a knitting needle to push the stuffing neatly into the shape.

BODY AND LEGS

3 With the right sides facing, pin the two body sections together and backstitch across the shoulders and down the side seams, leaving the neck, armholes, and bottom edge open.

4 In the same way, stitch the two legs together, turn right side out, and stuff. Pin the raw edges together and put to one side.

ASSEMBLING THE DOLL

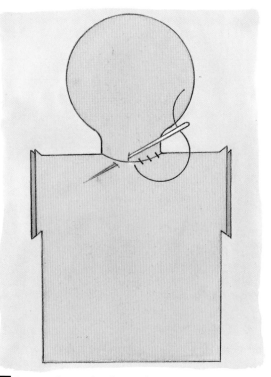

5 Turn in the neck edge of the unstuffed body and insert the neck of the stuffed head into the opening. Pin and, with matching thread, hand stitch around the neck, working extra stitches at the shoulder seam for extra strength.

Loops of black, brown and beige embroidery thread are used for the hair.

6 Insert the arms at an angle so that they point downward and stitch in place. This time, with reduced padding in the tops of the arms, use backstitch through all layers pulling the stitches firmly to make the "joint" more flexible.

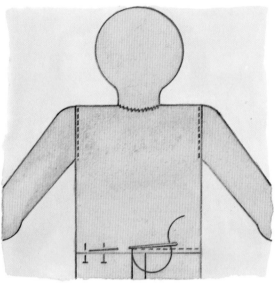

7 Now stuff the body to give a soft, evenly shaped finish. Pin the legs in position and stitch across in the same way as for the arms.

HAIR

8 Using the appropriate embroidery threads (black, brown, beige), work the hair as for the keepsake doll, see page 77. Work with two strands in the needle beginning with the brown thread. Add the black to create density and then work the beige loops for a highlighted effect. Continue to do this until the head is completely covered and the hairline around the face is well defined.

FACE AND FINGERS

9 Attach two old buttons for the eyes. Using red embroidery thread, suggest the mouth with stem stitch and the cheeks with stars made by crossing simple straight stitches. Apply the fingers to the hands with five straight stitches worked in brown embroidery thread.

CLOTHING PATTERN PIECES
FOR BOY

- Patterns for this project are full size and do not need to be enlarged. Before pinning on the pattern pieces, see the Checklist on page opposite.

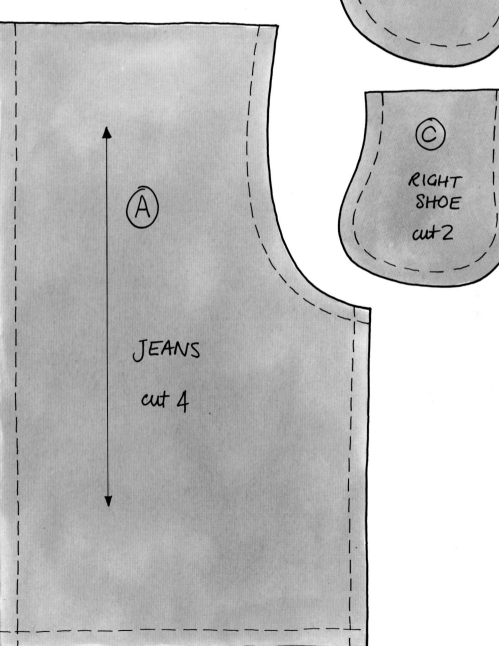

Ⓐ

JEANS

cut 4

Ⓑ LEFT SHOE cut 2

Ⓒ RIGHT SHOE cut 2

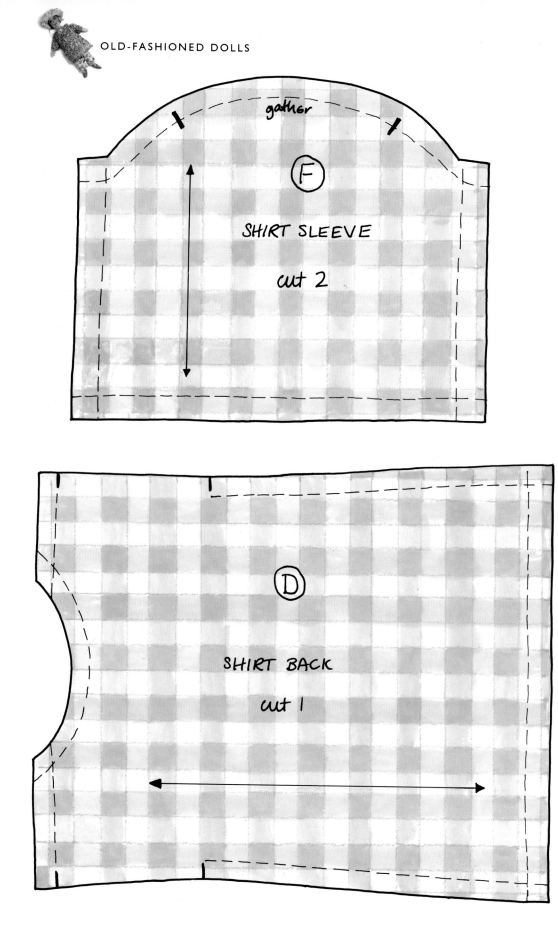

gather

Ⓕ

SHIRT SLEEVE

cut 2

Ⓔ

SHIRT
FRONT

cut 2

Ⓓ

SHIRT BACK

cut 1

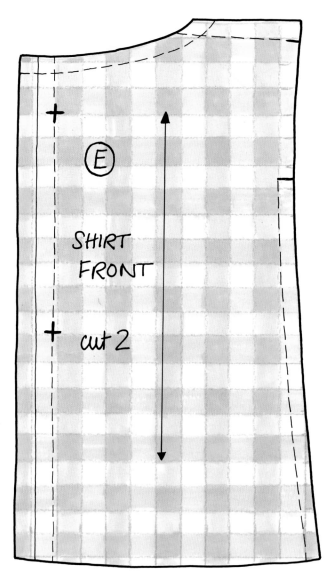

Other pattern pieces:
For the hat, make paper patterns
as follows and cut out of denim
fabric.
For the brim Ⓖ draw a circle 5in.
across with an inner circle 1½in.
across and cut out the inner circle.
For the hat top Ⓗ cut out another
circle 2½in. across.
For the hat band Ⓙ cut out a
rectangle 8¼in. x 2in.

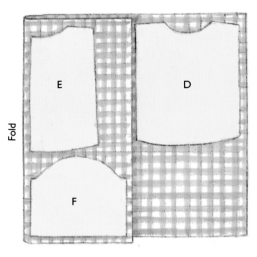

Cutting layout for small check fabric

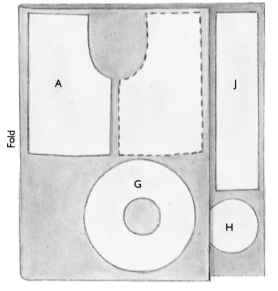

Cutting layout for old blue denim fabric

BOY'S CLOTHES ~ SHIRT

1 With the right sides together, pin the two shirt front pieces to the shirt back. Backstitch along the shoulder seams and side seams, taking a ¼in seam.

2 In the same way, join the two sleeve pieces and hand stitch along each underarm.

3 With the right sides together, pin the sleeves into the armholes of the shirt, easing the fullness of the sleeve cap to the top and back of the armhole and aligning the underarm seams with the side seams. Backstitch in place.

4 Make narrow double hems around the neckline, the bottom of the shirt, and along both shirt fronts, and then, with a contrasting thread, secure with running stitches of random length. Leave the bottom raw edge of the sleeves unstitched.

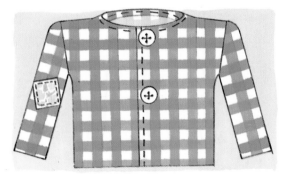

5 Attach the two snaps to the front of the shirt. Sew the two buttons on top of the snaps on the right side of the shirt. Stitch a little square of contrasting fabric to the arm of the shirt, to resemble a patch. Use contrasting thread and large stitches for a homespun look.

PANTS

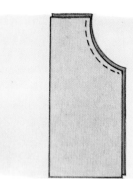

6 Place the four denim pants pieces into two pairs with right sides together. Pin and backstitch along the curved seam from the waist edge to the crotch on both sets of pants pieces.

7 Open up the two pants pieces and place them together with the right sides facing and the crotch seams matching. Backstitch all the way along the two inside leg seams. Similarly, backstitch the two outside leg seams.

8 Turn the pants right side out. Pull away loose threads at the waist and pants bottoms to encourage fraying. Take a tiny square of contrast fabric, turn under the raw edges, and hand stitch it to one leg of the pants to form a patch. Again, use contrasting thread and big stitches to secure the patch.

HAT

9 Pin the two hat brim pieces together with the wrong sides facing and, with a contrasting thread, overcast around the edge. Join together the two short edges of the hat band to form a circle. Press open the seam. Pin the "circle" inside the brim, right sides facing, and with the brim uppermost, backstitch in place. Turn to the wrong side.

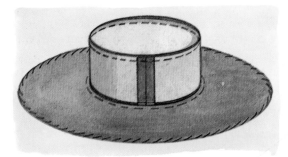

10 Pin the hat top piece to the hat band and, working with the top uppermost, backstitch in place. Turn the hat right side out.

BOOTS

11 Pin the four boot pieces together in pairs to make the two individual boots. With brown sewing thread in the needle, overcast around the edges working the stitches close together. Leave the top edge open.

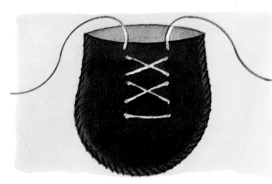

12 Following the diagram and using the lighter embroidery thread, stitch a shoelace pattern on the front of the boots. Leave enough thread in each boot to tie in a bow.

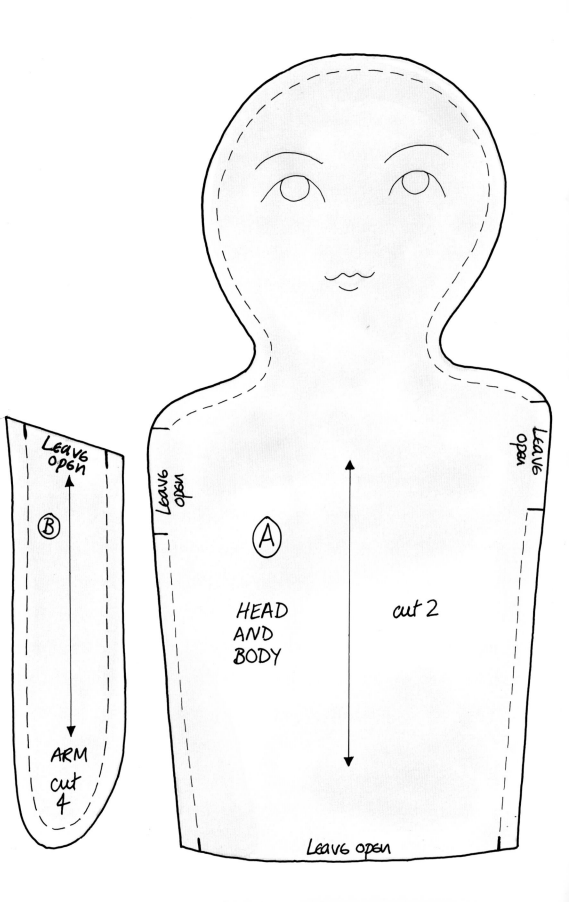

Leave open

B

Leave open

Leave open

A

cut 2

ARM
cut
4

HEAD
AND
BODY

Leave open

PATTERN PIECES FOR GIRL DOLL

- Patterns for this project are full size and
- do not need to be enlarged. Before
- pinning on the pattern pieces, see the
- Checklist on page 62.

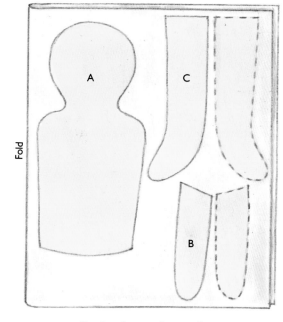

Cutting layout for muslin

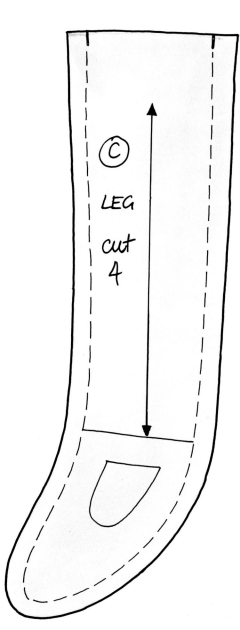

2 Use the end of a knitting needle to push out any tight corners. Stuff, beginning with the head. Again, you may need to use the end of the knitting needle to help push the stuffing well in to give a smooth, rounded shape. Turn in and pin the openings for the arms and then continue to stuff the body. Finger-press the turnings on the bottom opening and put the body to one side.

ARMS AND LEGS

3 With right sides together, pin the four arm pieces together to make two arms. Machine stitch around, leaving the opening for turning right side out, as shown on the pattern. Clip the curved seam allowance and turn right side out.

GIRL DOLL ~ HEAD AND BODY

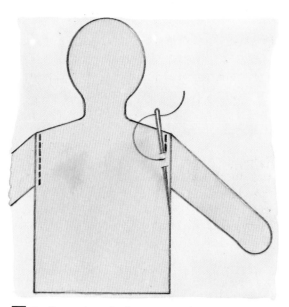

1 Pin the two head and body pieces right sides together, and machine stitch around, taking a ¼in seam. Leave the bottom edge open for turning right side out, and two openings at each side for the arms. Using small scissors, clip the curved seam allowance, just short of the stitches, and turn right side out.

4 Stuff evenly as before. Insert the arms into the body so that they are pointing downward (first removing the pins) and, with matching thread, backstitch through all four layers to secure.

5 Stitch the leg pieces together in the same way and stuff evenly. Place them inside the bottom edge of the body with the toes pointing outward. Pin and backstitch through all four layers, as for the arms.

HAIR

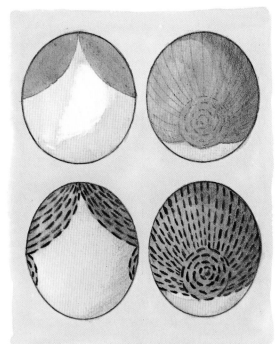

6 Following the diagram and working freehand, lightly draw in the hairline with a pencil. Then, with watered-down brown fabric paint and a brush, fill in the hair. Suggest the texture and direction of the hair with lines of running stitches using a darker brown embroidery thread as shown.

Designed to look handmade, the stitching does not have to look perfect on these dolls.

FACE

7 Working freehand, lightly draw in the features with a pencil, as shown in the diagram. Fill in the lips and cheeks with watered-down red fabric paint in two strengths; the palest for the cheeks. Outline the eyes and eyebrows with running stitches using one strand of brown embroidery thread. Work the eyes in satin stitch using two strands of blue.

SHOES

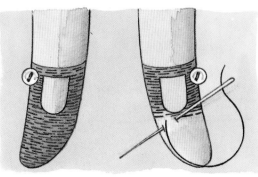

8 Lightly draw the outline as shown in the diagram and work the shoes with two strands of green embroidery thread using long and short filling stitches. Add the two pearl buttons to the side, as shown.

CLOTHING PATTERN PIECES
FOR GIRL

- Patterns for this project are full size and do not need to be enlarged. For the dress, tape the two pattern pieces together before cutting the fabric. Before pinning on the pattern pieces, see the Checklist on page 62.

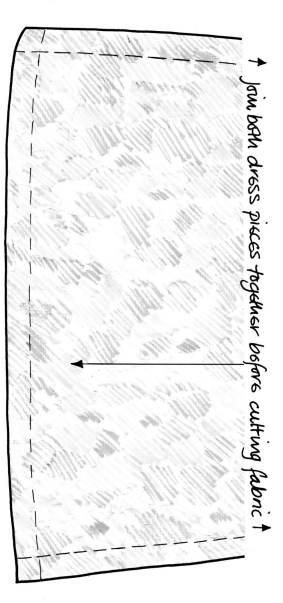

Join both dress pieces together before cutting fabric

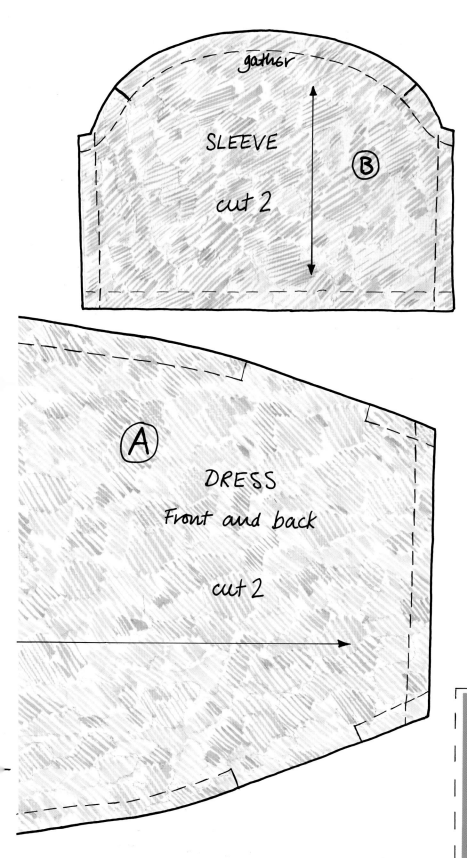

gather

SLEEVE

cut 2

Ⓑ

Ⓐ

DRESS

Front and back

cut 2

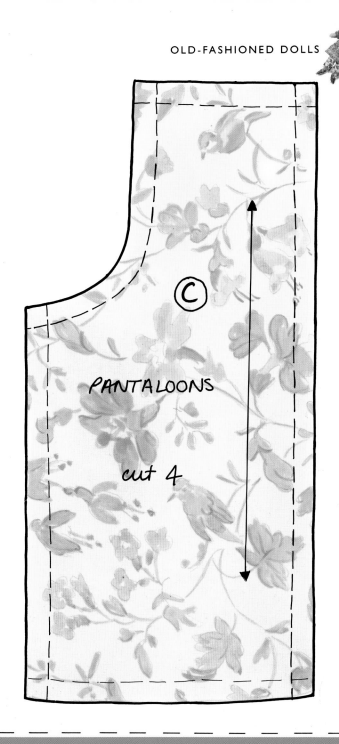

Ⓒ

PANTALOONS

cut 4

Other pattern pieces:

For the hat brim Ⓓ cut 2 circles 4in in diameter, with a central hole 1in in diameter, from the floral fabric.

For the hat top Ⓔ cut 1 circle 2in diameter.

For the hat band Ⓕ cut a piece 5½in x 1¼in

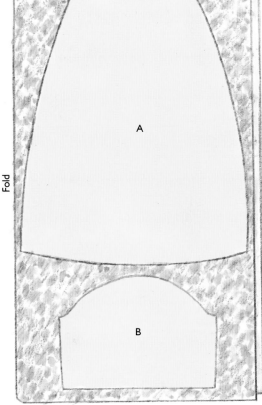

Fold

Cutting layout for lawn fabric

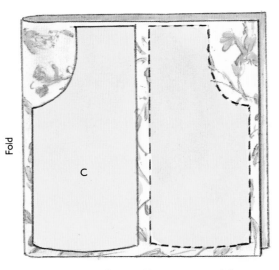

Fold

Cutting layout for small print cotton fabric

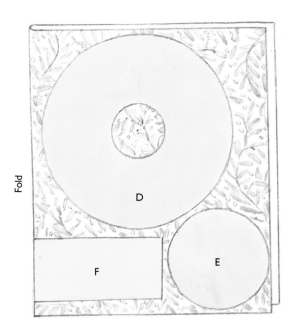

Fold

Cutting layout for contrasting printed pattern fabric

GIRL'S CLOTHES ~ DRESS

1 Pin the two dress pieces together with the right sides facing. Either hand sew (backstitch) or machine stitch along each side, leaving the armholes open about ½in down from the neck edge, as shown.

2 In the same way, join the underarm seams together on each sleeve, and press the seams open. Run a gathering thread around the sleeve cap and pull up the thread until the sleeve fits the armhole. Place the sleeves inside the dress with

the right sides together, aligning the seams and evening the gathers on the sleeve cap. Using matching thread, backstitch in place.

3 Decide which is the back of the dress and cut a 1½in opening from the neckline down the center back. Make narrow double hems on all the raw edges beginning with the back opening, then around the neck, sleeves, and the bottom of the dress. Using running stitches and matching sewing thread, pin and stitch to finish.

4 Turn under the short raw edges of the ½in-wide lace trim and attach it around the neck edge with neat running stitches. Apply the wider lace trim to the dress hem in the same way and, finally, attach a fabric or lace flower to the center front neck edge for decoration.

PANTALOONS

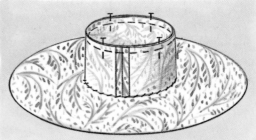

5 For each pair of pantaloons, pin the four pantaloon pieces together to make two legs and machine stitch around the curved edge taking a ¼in seam. Clip the seam allowance and press the seams open. Similarly, pin the two sections together and stitch around the inside leg seam in a continuous movement. Stitch the outside leg seams and finger-press all seams open.

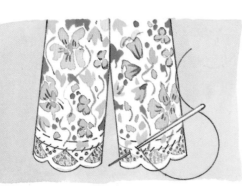

6 Make narrow double turnings on the waist edge and on the bottom of each leg and secure with tiny running stitches. Apply the lace trim to the inside of each leg and hemstitch it neatly to the hem. Overlap the raw edges of the trim, turn under, and secure with one or two stitches.

10 Pin the hat top to the hat band and, working from the wrong side with the top uppermost, backstitch in place. Turn to the right side, finger-pressing the seams flat.

HAT

7 With the right sides inside, pin the two hat brim pieces together and machine stitch around the outer edge. Trim and clip the seam allowance and turn right side out.

A fabric flower and old lace are pretty touches on the dress.

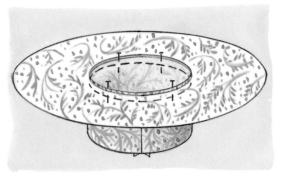

8 Similarly, join together the two short edges of the hat band to form a circle and open the seam. Fit the "circle" inside the brim, right sides facing, and pin the hat band and the top layer of the brim together. Backstitch in place.

9 Make a narrow hem on the brim lining, clip the edge if necessary, and slipstitch over the previous seam, to finish.

11 Apply the lace trim to the underside edge of the brim, neatly overlapping the raw edges of the lace and hemming in place. Attach the ribbon by overlapping the ends and stitching on the button to hold. Cut the ribbon ends as shown, to prevent fraying. To finish, apply one or two fabric flowers to the front of the hat stitching through the ribbon.

TURN YOUR MEMORIES INTO TOYS WITH THESE DELIGHTFUL KEEPSAKE DOLLS.

THEY MAKE THOUGHTFUL GIFTS FOR ADULTS AND OLDER CHILDREN ALIKE, AND

ARE AN IDEAL WAY OF MARKING A SPECIAL OCCASION.

Designed to look hand-made, these dolls are not at all difficult to make.

To create a genuine keepsake doll, you need some pieces of fabric, scraps of lace or ribbon, pieces of jewelry, or other tiny objects that have a sentimental appeal for you.

Scraps of fabric from wedding or christening gowns are ideal for keepsake dolls —as are beads and tiny brooches. Putting a pocket on the doll means you can find a home for a ring, a message, or a child's first tooth!

KEEPSAKE DOLLS

MATERIALS

GIRL DOLL (measures 8½in high)

BODY

- 6in × 12in of lightweight cotton fabric, such as lawn, for the body
- 6in × 8in of narrow-striped lightweight cotton fabric for the legs
- Loose synthetic stuffing or kapok
- Cold tea (optional)
- Stranded embroidery floss in red, brown, black, and blue for the shoes, hair, and face details

BLOUSE AND SKIRT

- 15½in × 9½in of lightweight cotton fabric with a small printed pattern
- 16in of old lace trim, approx ¾in wide, for the sleeve edges
- 12in of ½in-wide trim, such as that used for a wedding dress or christening gown, with sentimental value, to trim the skirt hem
- Green and blue embroidery thread
- Three press snaps
- Three tiny buttons for the blouse

BONNET AND PANTALOONS

- 13in × 9½in of lightweight cotton fabric with a contrasting tiny print pattern
- 14in of old lace trim, ½in wide

SHAWL

- 14in × 3½in of old lace with one decorative edge

JEWELRY

- A small brooch or other piece of jewelry (with sentimental value) to attach to the doll

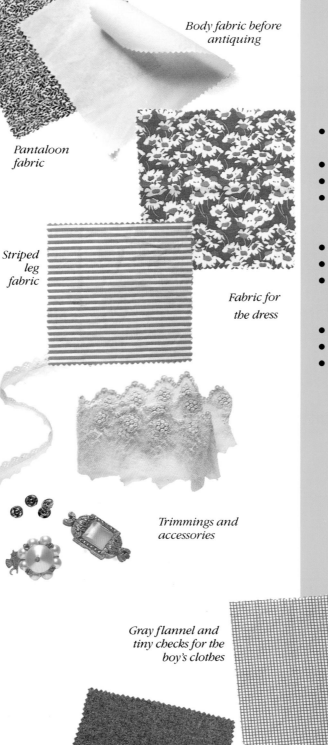

Body fabric before antiquing

Pantaloon fabric

Striped leg fabric

Fabric for the dress

Trimmings and accessories

Gray flannel and tiny checks for the boy's clothes

Embroidery threads

MATERIALS

BOY DOLL (measures 8½in high)

BODY

- 12in × 8½in of lightweight cotton fabric, such as lawn, for the body
- Synthetic stuffing or kapok
- Cold tea (optional)
- Embroidery threads in black, brown, red, and blue

SHIRT

- 7in × 9½in of mini-check or striped cotton fabric
- Two small snaps
- Two brown old buttons approx ¼in across

PANTS AND VEST

- 8½in × 10in of gray flannel or other similar fabric
- Two pearl buttons approx ⅜in across for the pants
- Green embroidery thread

DOLL PATTERN PIECES

- Patterns for this project are full size and do not need to be enlarged. Before pinning on the pattern pieces, see the Checklist on this page.

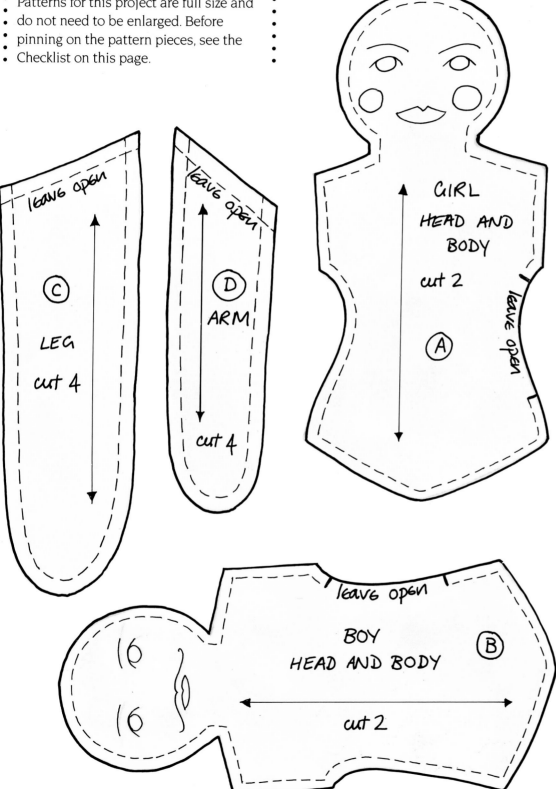

leave open

© C

LEG

cut 4

leave open

D ARM

cut 4

GIRL
HEAD AND
BODY

cut 2

Ⓐ

leave open

leave open

BOY
HEAD AND BODY

Ⓑ

cut 2

CHECKLIST

- Trace off the outline of the actual size pattern pieces, transfer all marks and cut out, see pages 6-7.
- Wash and press all new fabrics to test for shrinkage. "Antique" both the doll fabric and the clothes fabric, see page 6.
- Cut out the required number for each pattern piece from the appropriate fabric.
- Set your sewing machine to the correct stitch, length and tension and do a test run on your chosen fabric, see page 8.
- Seam allowances are included (except for the skirt, see step instructions) and should be stitched and trimmed back to ⅛in, see page 8.

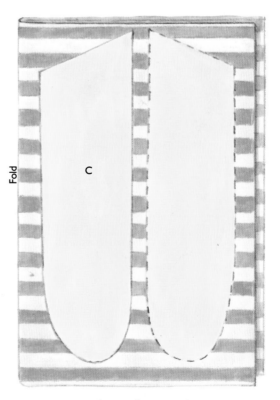

Fold

C

Cutting layout for striped cotton

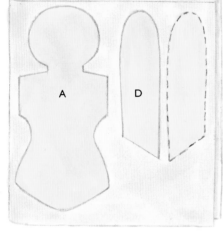

Cutting layout for lightweight cotton lawn

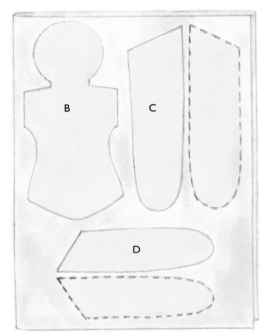

Cutting layout for white cotton

GIRL DOLL ~ HEAD AND BODY

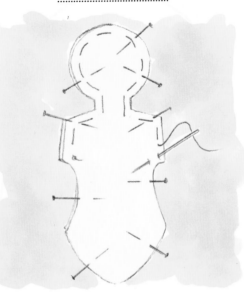

1 Pin and baste the two head and body pieces together with the right sides inside. Machine stitch the edges taking ¼in seams and leaving a 1in opening at one side of the body as shown on the pattern. Double-stitch down each side of the neck for extra strength.

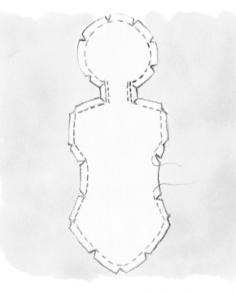

2 With small scissors, carefully clip the curved seam allowances at the neck and around the head and waist. Trim back the seams to ⅛in to reduce bulk around the head and neck.

3 Turn right side out using a knitting needle to help push out any awkward corners. If you want to give the doll an "antique" look simply dip the unstuffed pieces in cold tea and leave to dry before pressing them.

4 Stuff the body and head piece, starting with the head. Remember to tease out the stuffing and aim at a smooth finish and a well-shaped body and head. Use the end of a knitting needle to help push the stuffing well into the corners. Turn in the raw edges of the opening and, with matching sewing thread, neatly overcast to close.

ARMS AND LEGS

5 With the right sides inside, pin and baste the arm pieces together to make two arms. Machine stitch around taking a ¼in seam and leaving the short straight side open. Machine stitch the legs in the same way. Clip the curved seams, turn both the arms and legs right side out, and stuff.

Legs in a different fabric add a special touch to this doll.

6 Turn in the raw edges of the openings and, with matching sewing thread, overcast to close. It is important to turn under the edges evenly on both the arms and legs so they are the same length when finished.

7 Following the diagram for the correct position, attach both the legs and arms to the body using matching sewing thread and small overcasting stitches. Notice that the long side of the arm extends from the neck and forms the top of the arm and that the longer side of the leg extends from the hip and forms the outside of the leg.

HAIR

HAIR

8 Using two or three strands of brown embroidery thread in your needle, knot the end and stitch evenly all over the back of the head and around the face with small looped stitches. To work the stitch, make two backstitches into the same hole but, instead of pulling the first stitch through, leave a small loop. The loop is secured by the second stitch. Continue to sew loops to cover the entire head

FACE

9 For the face details, first mark out the eyes, eyebrows, lips, and cheeks with a very light pencil line as shown in the pattern. Using the appropriate colored embroidery threads, with a single strand in your needle, neatly embroider the eyes and cheeks in satin stitch, the lips and eyebrows in stem stitch, and outline the eyes and cheeks with backstitch. Take the needle to the back of the head to start and finish inside the hair.

SHOES

Boy shoe   Girl shoe

10 To embroider the shoes, first follow the diagram and lightly draw in the outline of the shoes onto the feet. Using red embroidery thread, fill in the shoe area with long and short stitch.

BOY DOLL ~ HEAD AND BODY

1 For the boy doll cut out the pattern pieces following the cutting layout and then continue to make the doll following the instructions for the girl memory doll until you are ready to embroider the face details and shoes.

2 For the boy's hair, use black embroidery thread and stitch looped backstitches to cover the head, as for the girl, see step 8.

3 For the face, embroider in exactly the same way as for the girl doll omitting her red cheeks and adding a black moustache filled in with rows of stem stitching (see the pattern).

4 Using black embroidery thread, embroider the shoes in the same way as for the girl but notice that the boy's shoes have a square buckle in front.

CLOTHING PATTERN PIECES
FOR GIRL

- Patterns for this project are full size and do not need to be enlarged. Pantaloon pattern piece is on page 83. Before pinning on the pattern pieces, see the checklist on page 75.

M PANTALOON DRAWSTRING

place on fold

B SKIRT WAISTBAND

cut 1

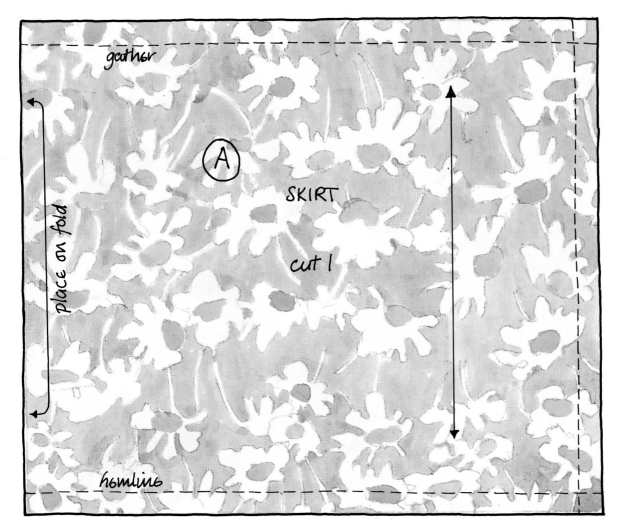

gather

place on fold

A

SKIRT

cut 1

hemline

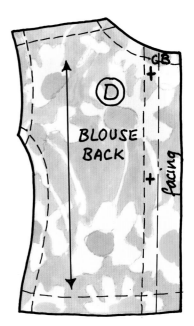

D BLOUSE BACK

CB

facing

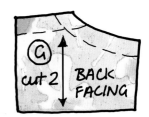

G cut 2 BACK FACING

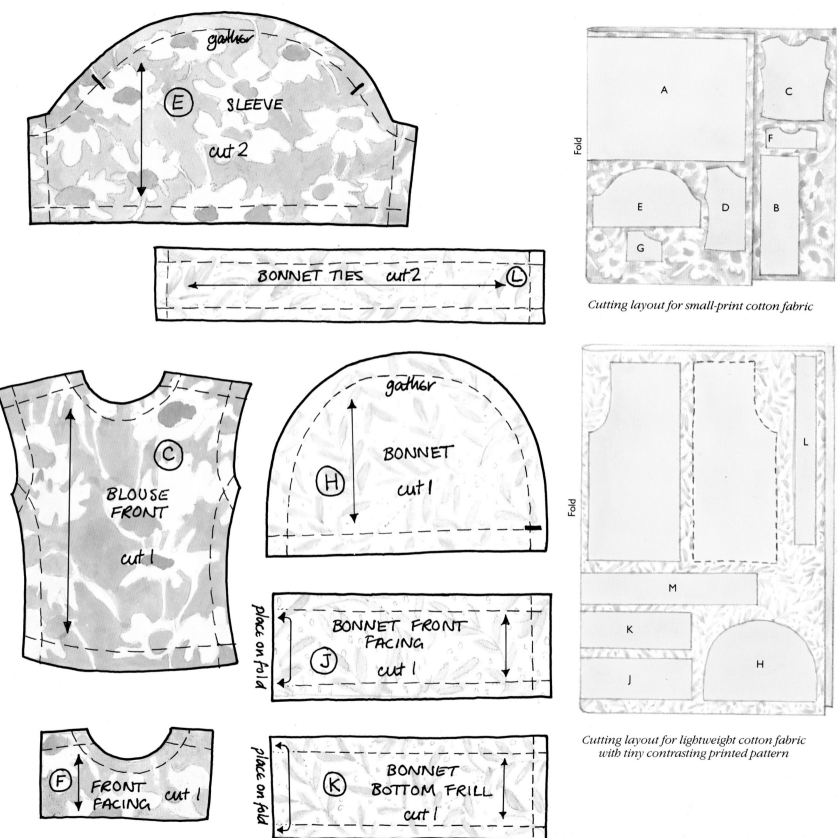

E SLEEVE cut 2 · gather

BONNET TIES cut 2 L

C BLOUSE FRONT cut 1

H BONNET cut 1 · gather

J BONNET FRONT FACING cut 1 · place on fold

F FRONT FACING cut 1

K BONNET BOTTOM FRILL cut 1 · place on fold

Cutting layout for small-print cotton fabric

A · C · F · E · D · B · G · Fold

Cutting layout for lightweight cotton fabric with tiny contrasting printed pattern

L · M · K · H · J · Fold

GIRL'S CLOTHES ~
PANTALOONS

1 For the pantaloons, use the trouser/pantaloon pattern piece on page 83. Pin the four leg pieces right sides together to make two legs. Baste and machine stitch along the curved edge. Clip the curved seam just short of the stitching and press the seam open. Repeat on the second leg.

2 With right sides inside, pin, baste, and machine stitch the two pieces together, stitching the inner leg seams in one continuous movement. Pin, baste, and machine stitch the two outer seams of the pantaloons. Press the seams open.

3 Press to the wrong side a ⁵⁄₁₆in double hem along the waist edge of the pantaloons and pin. Using matching sewing thread, stitch the hem.

4 Turn the pantaloons right side out and, using small scissors, make an upright slit through single fabric at the front of drawstring channel. Button-hole stitch around the slit to prevent it from fraying.

5 Make narrow double hems on each leg of the pantaloons and stitch, using matching sewing thread. Add the lace trim by hand, pinning to the wrong side of the leg hem and securing with small running stitches through a single layer of fabric. As an optional extra, you could decorate the pantaloon bottoms with a row of embroidery, such as chain stitch, feather stitch, or French knots, in a contrasting color.

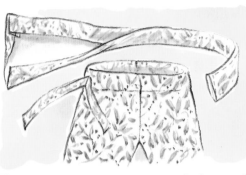

6 To make the drawstring, turn each short end of the fabric under ¼in and press. Fold each long side toward the center so that the two edges meet. Fold over once more and hand stitch to secure, using tiny running stitches. Attach a small safety pin to one end of the drawstring and thread it through the waist channel.

use the trouser/pantaloon pattern piece on page 83

BLOUSE

7 Pin the blouse front and the blouse front facing together, with the right sides inside and the necklines matching. Baste and then machine stitch around the neckline. Repeat on the two blouse back pieces.

8 Using small scissors, clip the seam allowance just short of the stitch line. Turn the facing to the wrong side and press the neck edge.

9 Pin the front and two back pieces right sides inside. Baste and machine stitch along the shoulder and side seams. Remove all basting stitches and press the seams open.

French knots, zigzag stitch, and feather stitch are used to decorate the clothes.

10 On each sleeve, pin and baste the two underarm edges together with the right sides inside, then machine stitch using matching sewing thread. Run a line of gathering stitches around the sleeve cap. Pull up the gathers so that the sleeve fits the armhole, and secure the thread. Even the gathers.

11 With right sides together, pin, baste and machine stitch the sleeves in place. You may find it easier to hand stitch the sleeves using tiny backstitches and matching thread. Clip the curved seams.

12 Make a double hem of ¼in on both sides of the back opening and neatly slipstitch. Attach two snaps: one at the neck and one at the waist, about 1in lower. Make a narrow hem on the bottom edge of the blouse and slipstitch around.

13 Similarly, turn up the edges of the sleeves and apply the lace trim to the wrong side. Cut the lace into two equal lengths and join the two short sides together to form two rings. Either gather or pleat the straight edge and pin to the sleeve. Adjust the gathers or pleats to fit and hand stitch in place with small running stitches. Repeat on the second sleeve.

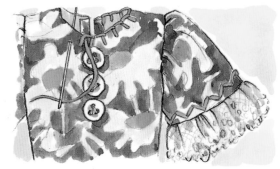

14 Sew the three buttons to the center front of the blouse. Using bright green embroidery thread, decorate around the sleeves with a row of zigzag stitch, and the neck with blanket stitch.

SKIRT

15 Working on the right side of the skirt section, pleat along one long edge making ¼in-deep pleats close together so that the pleated edge fits the waistband. Pin each pleat and baste inside the seam allowance using small stitches.

16 Fold the section right side inside and pin the center back seam together taking a ⅜in allowance. Baste and machine stitch up to the opening, about 1in from the waist edge. Press the seam open. Make narrow double hems on both sides of the opening and neatly hem using matching sewing thread.

17 With the right sides inside, pin the waistband to the waist edge of the skirt with the seam allowances extending beyond the opening. Baste and machine stitch in place.

18 Turn over the short edges of the waistband to the wrong side, taking ¼in hems, and press. Fold the waistband in half, make a single ¼in hem on the long edge, and pin it to the wrong side of the waistband. Using matching thread, hem in place, catching in the previous machine stitching.

To make the shawl, you could use scraps from a christening gown or bridal veil.

19 For the hem, fold over a narrow ⅛in turn and then a ¼in turn. Pin, and slipstitch with matching sewing thread. Working on the wrong side, attach the lace trim to the outer edge of the hem with running stitches, neatly overlapping the raw edge to finish.

20 Using bright green embroidery thread, add a border of feather stitching to finish the hem. Decorate the waistband with a row of bright blue French knots spaced ¼in apart. Stitch the snap to the waistband to close the opening.

BONNET

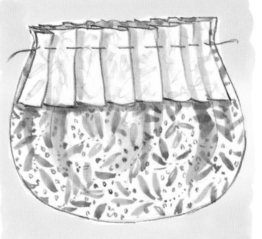

21 Run a line of gathering stitches along the bottom of the bonnet, gently gather, and secure the thread. Place the bonnet ruffle right sides together along the bottom of the bonnet; pleat to fit the gathered edge of the bonnet. Stitch the ruffle in place. Make a single turn to the wrong side along the bottom and press the ruffle downward.

22 Make a line of small gathering stitches along the curved edge of the main bonnet piece. Pull up the gathers to fit the front facing section. Secure the thread firmly

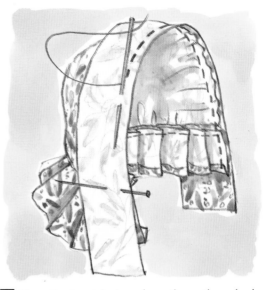

23 Place the front facing along the gathered edge of the bonnet, with right sides together and the edges aligned. There should be ¼in left over at each end to turn under. Hand stitch using small running stitches. Turn the front facing to the wrong side of the bonnet. Make a narrow hem and neatly slipstitch to hold.

24 Using tiny running stitches, attach lace trim along the bottom edge of the ruffle turning under the two raw edges of trim to finish. To make the ties, simply fold over the two long edges so that they meet in the middle. Fold over once more and hand stitch, turning under each end and securing with one or two stitches. Attach one tie to each side of the bonnet with small stitches. Add a line of embroidery stitches to the front band of the bonnet, using French knots, zigzag stitch, or chain stitch as preferred.

SHAWL AND JEWELRY

25 The ideal lace edging will have deep decorative scallops or points and a fine mesh ground. Simply make a narrow hem on each short edge and a similar one on the neck edge. Gather this edge to fit around your doll and secure the thread. Attach a favorite brooch to fasten at the neck or a length of pearl necklace, as shown here.

CLOTHING PATTERN PIECES
FOR BOY

- Patterns for this project are full size and
- do not need to be enlarged. Before
- pinning on the pattern pieces, turn to the
- Checklist on page 75.

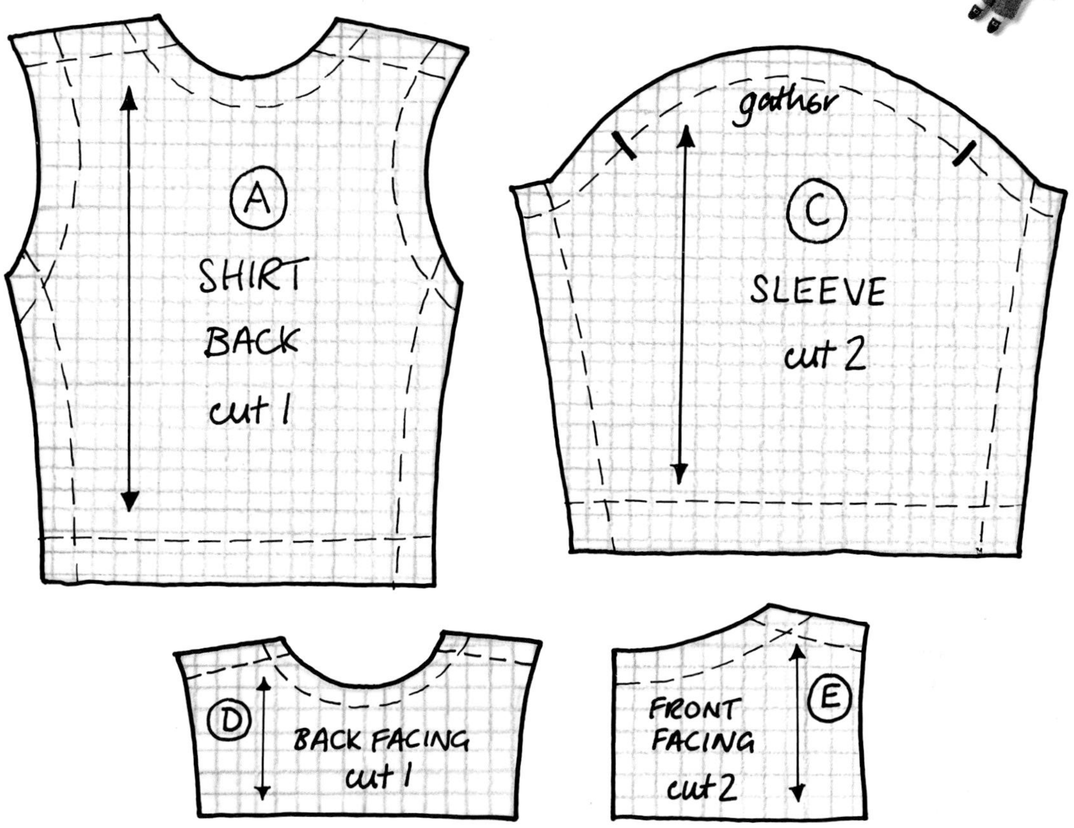

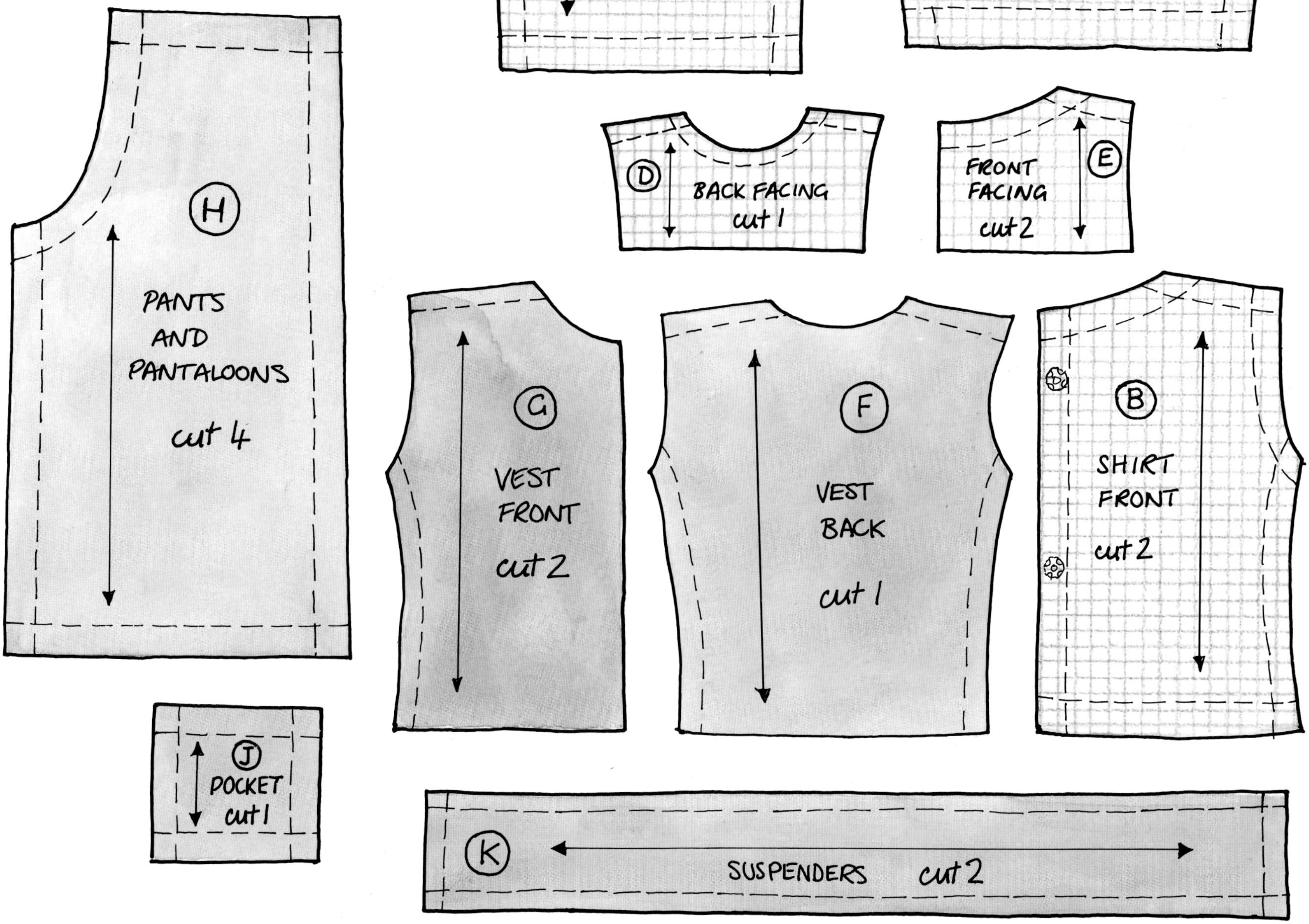

Ⓐ SHIRT BACK cut 1

Ⓒ SLEEVE cut 2
gather

Ⓓ BACK FACING cut 1

Ⓔ FRONT FACING cut 2

Ⓗ PANTS AND PANTALOONS cut 4

Ⓖ VEST FRONT cut 2

Ⓕ VEST BACK cut 1

Ⓑ SHIRT FRONT cut 2

Ⓙ POCKET cut 1

Ⓚ SUSPENDERS cut 2

BOY'S CLOTHES ~ SHIRT

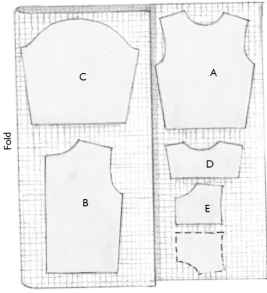

Cutting layout for mini-check fabric

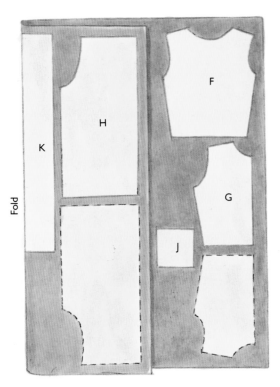

Cutting layout for gray flannel

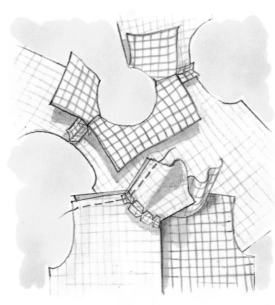

1 With right sides together, place the back facing onto the shirt back section with the edges of the neck and shoulders matching. Hand stitch around the neckline with small running stitches. Do the same on both shirt fronts.

2 Clip the curved seam allowance just short of the stitching, and turn the facings to the wrong side. Press the neck edge. Place the two shirt fronts onto the shirt back with the right sides together. Lift up the facings and handsew along the facing, shoulder seams and side seams.

3 Join together the underarm seams on both sleeves using running stitches. Finger-press the seams open. Insert the sleeves into the armhole with the right sides inside, aligning the underarm sleeve with the side seam of the shirt. Ease with tiny gathers or pleats, if necessary and, using tiny running stitches, hand sew in place.

4 Turn under and stitch with small running stitches the bottom edge of the shirt, then do the same for the two front seams and the sleeves.

For the hair, black embroidery thread is sewn in loops.

5 Attach two snaps to the front of the shirt about 1in apart and then sew the two buttons on top.

Bright green embroidery thread is used to work blanket stitch around the jacket edges.

PANTS

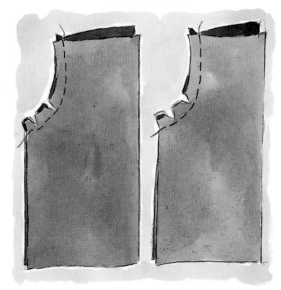

6 With right sides together, join the four pants leg pieces together to make two legs. Pin and hand stitch around the curved seam using small running stitches. Clip the curved seam and finger-press the seam open.

7 Place the two leg sections together right sides inside. Hand stitch the inside leg seams in one continuous operation. Stitch the two side seams and press the seams open.

8 Finish the waist edge and pants legs by making a single ¼in hem and hand stitching into place using bright green embroidery thread and running stitches.

9 To make the suspenders, fold the two lengths over and using bright green embroidery thread, stitch down the middle of each one. Attach the suspenders to the inside waist edge of the pants at the front and back, with a crossover at the back. Use one or two small stitches to secure.

10 Sew the two pearl buttons to the right side of the pants where the suspenders are stitched. Stitch across the top edge of the pocket and pin in place. Turn under these remaining sides and stitch. You can keep something of sentimental value in the memory doll's pocket, for example, your baby's first tooth.

VEST

11 Place the two front pieces on the back piece with the shoulder and side seams matching, and with right sides together. Using matching sewing thread, hand stitch to secure. Finger-press the seams open.

12 Using bright green embroidery thread, work blanket stitch around the outside edges and both armholes to finish and decorate the vest. Because flannel is so thick, the edges, as in this case, can be decorated as a single layer without making hems.

ANGEL ON MY PILLOW

Folk-art fabrics have been used to make this delightful angel. Whatever materials you choose, this pajama-case doll is sure to become a treasured toy kept safely tucked up in a child's bed.

The bottom of the angel's skirt can be opened and closed so nightclothes can be stored inside. If you are making her as a gift for a young child who may want to cuddle the doll, choose soft, wooly hair. For an older girl or teenager, raffia hair makes her an unusual mascot – especially with a little heart popped in her pinafore pocket.

Fabric for the wings and little heart

Cotton jersey for the body.

Fabric for the pinafore

Fabric for the case and ruffle

Dress fabric

Sleeve fabric

MATERIALS

DOLL (measures 20in high)
- 18in of 44in-wide cotton jersey for the body
- Synthetic stuffing or kapok
- One skein of raffia for the hair
- Blusher and black felt-tipped pen for the face details

CLOTHES AND CASE
- Large chenille needle
- 18in of 44in-wide of large white spot cotton for the case, outside pocket, and pinafore ruffle
- 18in of 44in-wide of red stripe cotton for the pinafore and inside pocket
- 18in of 44in-wide of tiny check cotton for the dress
- 9in of 44in-wide of polkadot cotton for the sleeves
- 9in of 44in-wide red-spotted cream cotton for the wings and heart
- 15in × 10in of heavyweight interfacing for the wings
- 18in of velcro fastening for the case
- Two large snaps to secure the wings to the body
- 1yd of harmonizing ⅜in-wide ribbon to trim the wings and heart
- 18in of ⅛in-wide ribbon for the dress neck

Ribbon trims and raffia – don't use raffia if you are making this doll for a young child; use yarn instead

PATTERN PIECES FOR BODY AND CASE

Patterns for this project should be enlarged to twice the size. If you have access to a photocopier with an enlarging facility, set it to 200%. Otherwise, trace the patterns on a grid, following the procedure outlined on page 7. (See also the Checklist on this page).

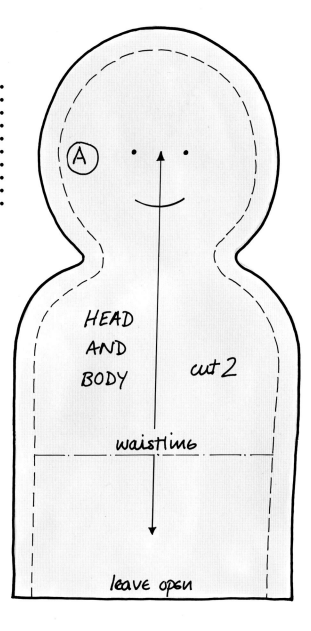

A

HEAD AND BODY   cut 2

waistline

leave open

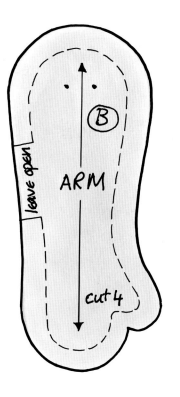

B

leave open

ARM

cut 4

Other pattern pieces:
For the pajama case Ⓒ cut one
piece 14in x 36in on the
straight grain from the large
white spot fabric.

CHECKLIST

- Enlarge the pattern pieces. Transfer all marks and cut out, see pages 6-7.
- Wash and press the main fabrics, see page 6.
- Cut out the required number for each pattern piece from the appropriate fabric, see page 7.
- Set your sewing machine to the correct stitch, length and tension and do a test run on your chosen fabric, see page 8.
- Seam allowances are included throughout. Unless otherwise stated, stitch and trim back to ¼in, snip into curved seams and press open, see page 8.

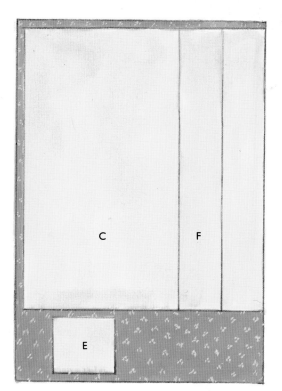

C

F

E

Cutting layout for red/white spot fabric

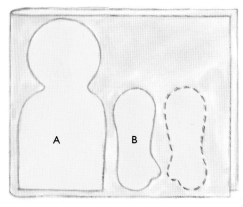

A

B

Cutting layout for cotton jersey

*Back view
of the wings*

ARMS

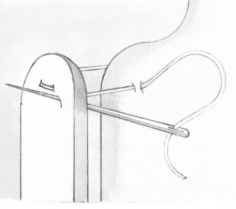

2 Pin the four arm pieces together, with right sides facing, in pairs. Machine stitch around leaving an opening as shown. Trim and clip the seams before turning right side out. Insert the filling, turn in the raw edges of the opening, and overcast to close. Using the chenille needle, sew the arms to the body by hand at the points marked on the pattern.

THE BODY AND CASE ~
BODY

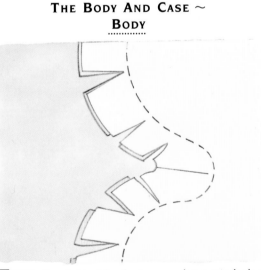

1 With the right sides facing, machine stitch the two body pieces together on the stitching line leaving the bottom edge open as shown. Trim and clip the seams where necessary and turn right side out. Turn in and baste the seam allowance along the opening. Insert the filling using a knitting needle to push it evenly into the head and body. Overcast the opening to close.

FACE AND HAIR

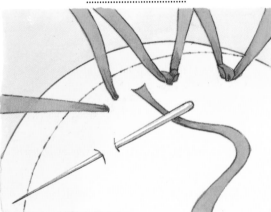

3 Using a fine black felt-tipped pen, mark the eyes as shown on the pattern. Suggest the cheeks by brushing the face lightly with blusher. To make the hair, cut the raffia into uneven lengths of about 5in and, with the chenille needle, thread each length separately through the fabric, working around the face and over the back of the head. Knot the ends firmly together to hold each length in place and space the strands evenly to cover the head. The mouth can be embroidered or drawn on.

CASE

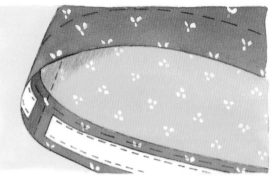

4 With right sides facing, machine stitch the two short sides together to make the side seam of the case. Press the seam open. Turn up and baste a 1in hem along one long edge. Cut the velcro to measure about 1in less than half the width of the case. Machine stitch one of the strips to the back and one to the front of the hem edge, stitching along both sides of the tape. About 3in from the waist edge, stitch a line across the top of the case (through both layers) to form a pocket for the body of the doll.

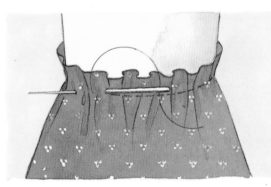

5 Using a long machine stitch, run a row of gathering stitches along the waist edge of the case. Pull up the gathers until they fit around the waist of the doll and then backstitch the case to the doll along the waistline, as marked.

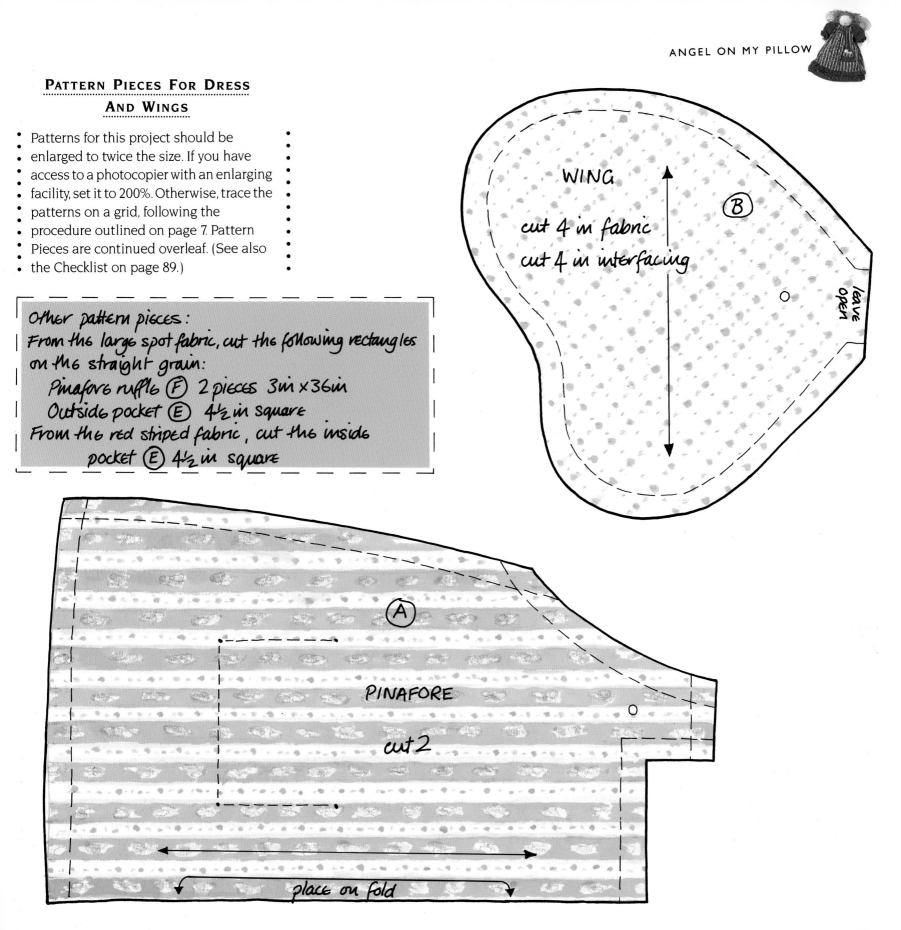

PATTERN PIECES FOR DRESS AND WINGS

Patterns for this project should be enlarged to twice the size. If you have access to a photocopier with an enlarging facility, set it to 200%. Otherwise, trace the patterns on a grid, following the procedure outlined on page 7. Pattern Pieces are continued overleaf. (See also the Checklist on page 89.)

Other pattern pieces:
From the large spot fabric, cut the following rectangles on the straight grain:
Pinafore ruffle (F) 2 pieces 3in x 36in
Outside pocket (E) 4½ in square
From the red striped fabric, cut the inside pocket (E) 4½ in square

WING
cut 4 in fabric
cut 4 in interfacing
(B)
leave open

PINAFORE
cut 2
(A)
place on fold

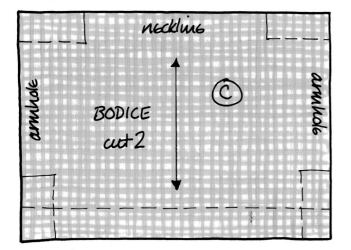

neckline

armhole

armhole

BODICE
cut 2

C

Other pattern pieces:

For the dress skirt G cut one rectangle on the straight grain 4 in X 36 in from the tiny check cotton.

HEART

cut 2

leave open

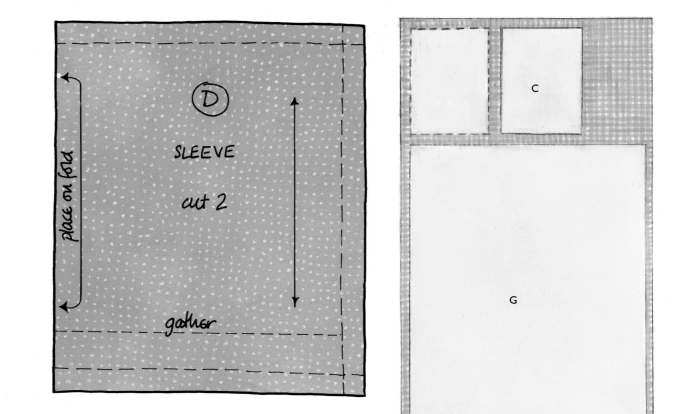

place on fold

D

SLEEVE

cut 2

gather

C

G

Cutting layout for tiny check fabric

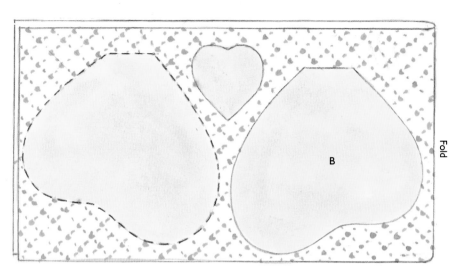

Cutting layout for white/red spot fabric

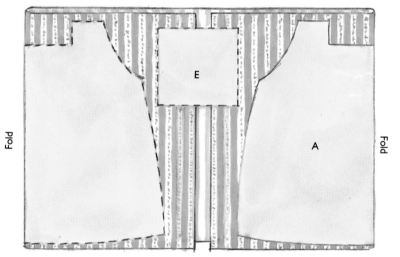

Cutting layout for red and cream stripe
Pocket cut from single layer only

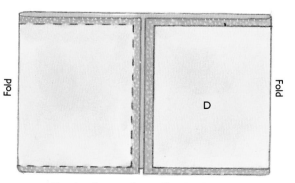

Cutting layout for polkadot fabric

THE DRESS AND WINGS ~
DRESS

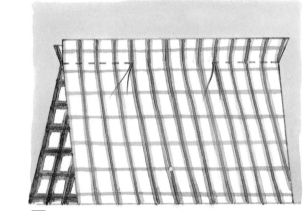

1 Machine stitch the shoulder seams of the bodice together, with the right sides facing, and leaving the neckline open. Press the shoulder seams open and the seam allowance of the neck to the inside.

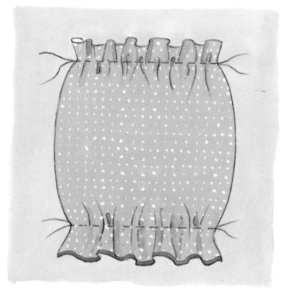

2 Using a long machine stitch, run a row of gathering stitches along the top edge of the sleeve. Turn in and machine stitch a ¼in hem along the lower wrist edge. Make a second row of gathering stitches ¾in in from the hem.

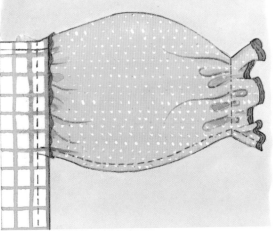

PINAFORE

3 Pull up the gathers on the sleeve cap until it is the same length as the armhole between the notches. Then, with the right sides facing, stitch the sleeve to the bodice armhole. Similarly, stitch the side seams of the bodice and the underarm seam of the sleeve in a continuous movement.

4 Working on the wrong side, stitch the short sides of the skirt piece together and press the seam open. Make a row of gathering stitches along one raw edge of the skirt, just inside the seam allowance, and a ½in hem along the other. Pull up the gathers until the skirt fits the bodice waistline. With the right sides facing, machine stitch the skirt to the bodice.

5 Put the dress on the doll and, using a fairly long running stitch, sew narrow ribbon around the neck about ¼in from the edge. Pull up the stitches until the neck fits the doll and tie with a bow in the center front. Pull up the gathers at the wrist edge of the sleeves and fasten off securely.

6 Run a row of gathering stitches along the neckline of the back and front pinafore pieces. Pull up the gathers on each piece to a length of 2¼in. With the right sides facing, stitch the shoulder seams together and open the seam. Carefully clip the corners of the neckline, make a narrow single hem all around, and machine stitch in place.

This homespun angel could also be made up in fabrics to match your bed linen.

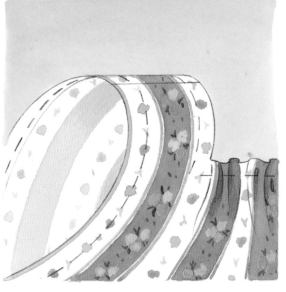

7 With the right sides facing, stitch the side seams together and press them open. Finish the armholes with a single hem and machine stitch around.

MAKING THE WINGS

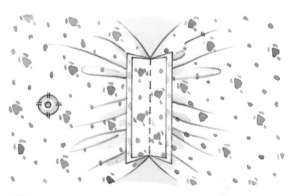

8 Working on the wrong side, stitch the two ruffle pieces together along both short sides. Turn to the right side, fold the strip in half lengthwise and run a row of gathering stitches through both layers just inside the seamline. Pull the gathers until the ruffle is the same size as the hem of the pinafore. With both right sides facing, stitch the ruffle to the hem and then press the seam allowances up.

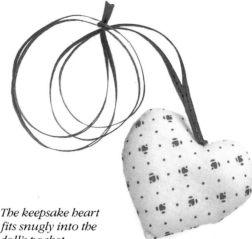

The keepsake heart fits snugly into the doll's pocket.

KEEPSAKE HEART

11 Using herringbone stitch, attach one piece of interfacing to the wrong side of each of two wing pieces and then, with right sides inside, pin the four wing pieces together to make one pair of wings. Machine stitch around leaving an opening as marked on the pattern. Turn right side out, press, and join the two wings together by machine stitching along the center seam. Tie the ribbon tightly around the seam to cover the join.

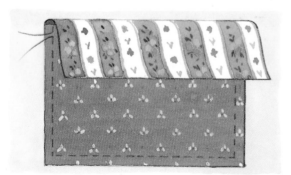

9 With the right sides facing, stitch the two pocket pieces together, leaving a 1½in opening on one side for turning after sewing. Press and slipstitch the opening closed. With the wrong side of the pocket to the right side of the pinafore, pin the pocket in place as shown on the pattern. Stitch around to within 1in of the top edge so that the pocket flap can be folded over to the right side.

10 With right sides inside, stitch the two heart pieces together taking a ¼in seam and leaving an opening for turning right side out. Stuff evenly and overcast the opening to close. Using tiny hemming stitches, attach a 4in length of ribbon to the center top of the heart to form a loop. The heart can then easily be removed from the pocket or hung around the doll's wrist.

12 To secure the wings, sew a half snap to the underside of each wing and the matching half to the back shoulder strap of the pinafore on each side, as shown on the pattern.

OVERALLS, PANTALOONS, AND

PETTICOATS — THE COUNTRY

COUSINS HAVE PUT ON THEIR

CITY CLOTHES AND WILL MAKE A

CONVERSATION PIECE SITTING

IN YOUR COUNTRY-STYLE KITCHEN.

COUNTRY COUSINS

Separate pattern pieces for the arms and legs and clever finger detailing guarantee that the country cousins are very attractive dolls while still being easy to make.

The clothes are simple but stylish: the boy has on a new pair of overalls with a bow tie and matching handkerchief to dress it up for Sunday best; the little girl has a floral print dress and matching lacy pantaloons and petticoat.

Choose your own colors for the hair and clothes, perhaps to match the decor in one of your rooms, as you are bound to want to display this charming pair.

MATERIALS

DOLLS (measure 20in high)

- 1yd of 44in-wide muslin for the two bodices
- Synthetic stuffing or kapok
- 2oz of bulky knitting yarn for the girl's hair
- 2oz of knitting worsted yarn for the boy's hair
- 18in of ½in-wide fabric tape to match the hair color of your choice
- Four safety plastic eyes
- 1yd of ¾in-wide ribbon in a contrasting color for girl doll's hair
- Black and red fine felt-tipped pens and pink blusher for the face details
- Fabric glue

BOY'S PANTS

- 18in of 36in-wide denim fabric
- Two mini snaps

BOY'S SHIRT

- 18in of 36in-wide narrow-stripe cotton fabric
- 7in of ½in-wide bias binding to match
- Four small buttons approx ⅜in across
- 18in of ½in-wide elastic
- Three snaps ⅜in across

BOY'S BOWTIE AND HANKY

- 8in square of floral print cotton fabric
- 9in length of round elastic
- 5in square of fabric to match the bowtie

BOY'S BOOTS

- 10in square of soft leather
- 2yds of thick crochet cotton for the laces

Muslin

Fabrics for boy's clothes

Knitting yarn for hair

Fabrics for girl's clothes

Felt and leather

Safety eyes, buttons, and braid for laces

GIRL'S UNDERSKIRT AND PANTALOONS

- 12in of 60in-wide white cotton eyelet lace
- 20in of ⅛in-wide elastic
- 2yds of white eyelet lace trim, 1¼in wide

GIRL'S DRESS

- 18in of 36in-wide cotton with small floral print
- Four small buttons, approx ⅜in across
- Three snaps, ¼in across
- Shirring elastic

GIRL'S BOOTS

- 8in square of felt
- 1yd of thin braid for the laces

DOLL PATTERN PIECES

Patterns for this project should be enlarged to twice the size. If you have access to a photocopier with an enlarging facility, set it to 200%. Otherwise, trace the patterns on a grid, following the procedure outlined on page 7. (See also the Checklist on this page).

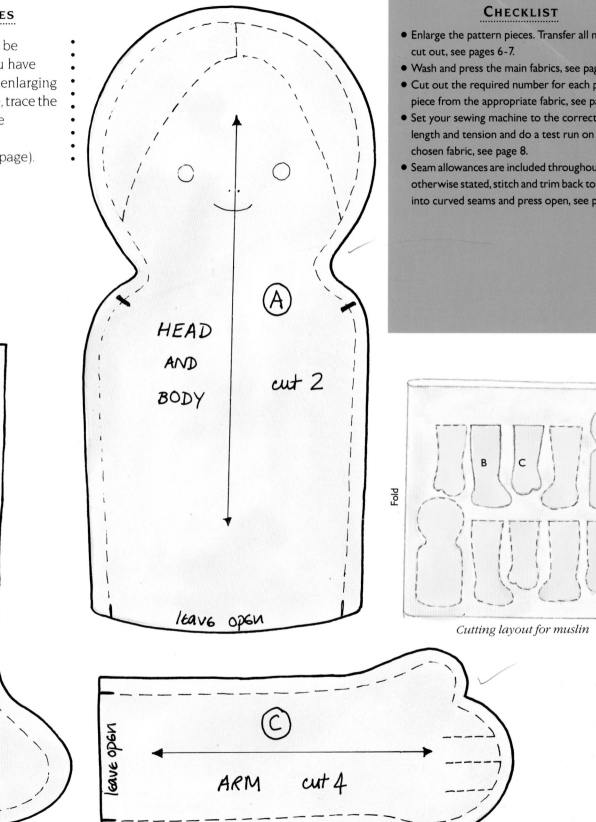

leave open

Ⓐ

HEAD

AND

BODY

cut 2

leave open

Ⓑ

LEG

cut 4

leave open

Ⓒ

ARM   cut 4

CHECKLIST

- Enlarge the pattern pieces. Transfer all marks and cut out, see pages 6-7.
- Wash and press the main fabrics, see page 6.
- Cut out the required number for each pattern piece from the appropriate fabric, see page 7.
- Set your sewing machine to the correct stitch, length and tension and do a test run on your chosen fabric, see page 8.
- Seam allowances are included throughout. Unless otherwise stated, stitch and trim back to ¼in, snip into curved seams and press open, see page 8.

Fold

B   C   A

Cutting layout for muslin

99

THE DOLL ~
BODY AND HEAD

1 Pin, baste, and machine stitch the two head and body pieces together with the right sides facing and leaving the lower edge open where indicated on the pattern. Turn over the seam allowance of the opening and press with your fingers.

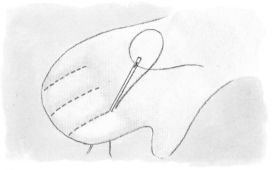

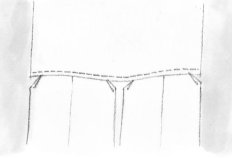

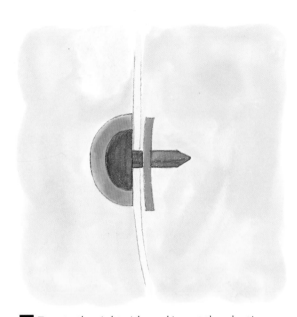

2 Turn to the right side and insert the plastic eyes into the fabric in the positions shown, securing them firmly at the back with the manufacturer's safety locking device as supplied. Stuff the head and body evenly, using a large knitting needle to help push the filling in place.

LEGS

3 Pin, baste, and machine stitch the leg pieces with the right sides together to form two pairs, leaving the top edge open as indicated on the pattern. Turn the legs right side out and stuff to within 1in of the top.

4 Bring the two seams together at the center of the leg and make an inverted pleat on each side so that the legs will fit easily into the base of the body. Pin the legs in position and then baste and machine stitch across.

ARMS

5 Pin, baste, and machine stitch the four arm pieces together to form two pairs, leaving the top edge open as shown on the pattern. Turn over the seam allowance of the opening and finger-press.

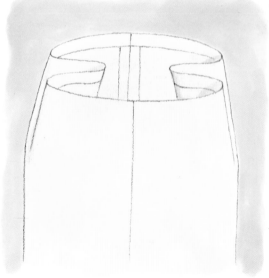

6 Turn the arms right side out and stuff to within 1in of the top. Make an inverted pleat at the top of the arm as shown and then overcast the edges together by hand. Pin the arms to the body as shown on the pattern and overcast by hand.

7 Define the fingers by backstitching along the finger lines as shown on the pattern. Complete the face by drawing in two tiny nostrils using black felt pen, the mouth in red pen, and suggest the cheeks with a light dusting of pink blusher.

BOY'S HAIR

8 Cut enough 10in lengths of yarn to cover the head thickly. Lay the yarn in parallel strands across the 5in length of tape leaving ½in at each end. Machine stitch the yarn to the tape.

9 Cut several 5in lengths of yarn for the bangs and glue these first to the center of the head with the ends hanging unevenly over the forehead.

10 Apply glue to the tape and then cover the glued ends of the bangs with the tape allowing it to run from the top of the head to the neckline. Trim the yarn to the required length and glue it to the neckline and to the hairline around the face.

Hair: front and back view.

GIRL'S HAIR

11 For the bangs cut about 20 lengths of yarn 6in long. Using a length of yarn, tie them together in the center and glue into position in the middle of the head. Trim the ends to uneven lengths and unravel some of the yarn to give a curled effect.

12 Cut about 80 lengths of yarn 26in long and tie them together in the center. Machine stitch the yarn onto a 5in length of tape using a long machine stitch. Place the tape along the center back of the head behind the bangs and glue in place.

13 Bring the strands forward and glue in place along the hairline around the face and neck. Cut some of the strands near the face short and plait the remaining lengths. Secure each braid with a ribbon bow and stitch it in place.

14 Cut 40 lengths of yarn 8in long and tie them together in the center. Glue the center of the hank to the top of the head behind the bangs and then trim and unravel as before.

CLOTHING PATTERN PIECES
FOR BOY

- Patterns for this project should be enlarged to twice the size. If you have access to a photocopier with an enlarging facility, set it to 200%. Otherwise, trace the patterns on a grid, following the procedure outlined on page 7. (See also the Checklist on page 99).

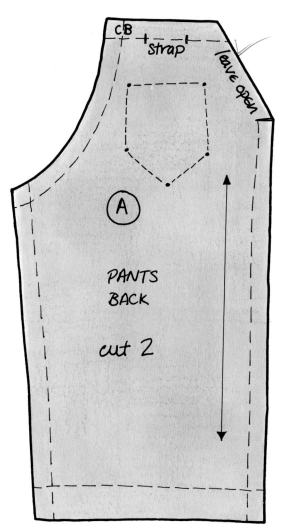

CB
strap
leave open
Ⓐ
PANTS BACK
cut 2

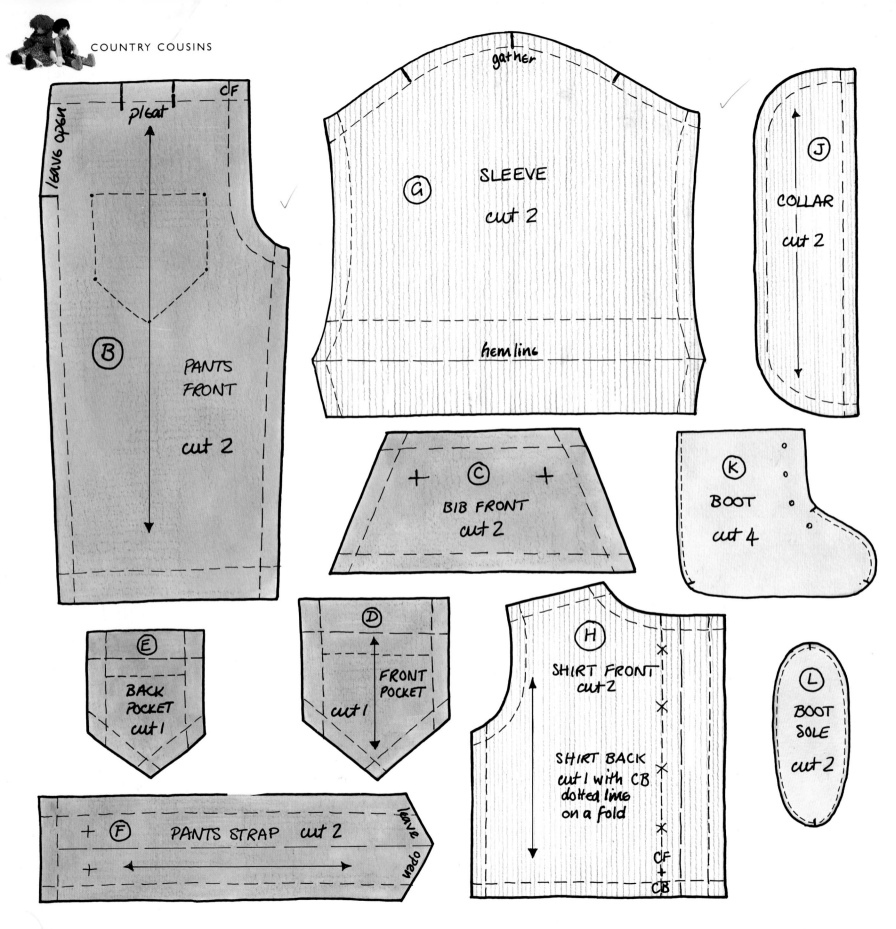

leave open

CF
pleat

B

PANTS
FRONT

cut 2

gather

G   SLEEVE

cut 2

hemline

J

COLLAR

cut 2

C

BIB FRONT
cut 2

K

BOOT

cut 4

E

BACK
POCKET
cut 1

D

FRONT
POCKET

cut 1

H

SHIRT FRONT
cut 2

SHIRT BACK
cut 1 with CB
dotted line
on a fold

CF

CB

L

BOOT
SOLE

cut 2

F   PANTS STRAP   cut 2

leave open

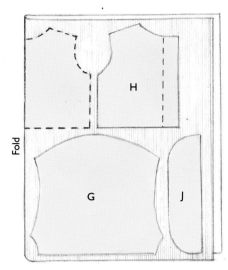

Cutting layout for narrow-striped fabric

Fold

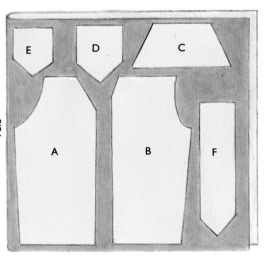

Cutting layout for denim fabric

Fold

The bow tie and pocket handkerchief match the girl doll's dress.

THE BOY'S CLOTHES ~ SHIRT

1 Pin, baste, and machine stitch the back and front shoulder seams together with the right sides inside. Press the seams open. With the right sides facing, stitch the collar pieces together around the outer curved edge only. Trim, snip into the curved seam, and turn right side out. Press and topstitch ⅛in from the finished edge.

2 Pin and baste the wrong side of the collar to the right side of the shirt neckline between the center front notches. Baste the bias binding on top of the collar, matching the seam lines, and then machine stitch through all thicknesses. Turn the binding over the raw edge of the neckline and hemstitch to the machine stitching on the wrong side.

3 On each shirt front, turn the facing to the right side along the fold line and stitch across the remaining neckline. Turn to the wrong side and press the fold lines.

4 Gather the sleeve cap between the notches as shown in the diagram and also along the wrist edge, using a long machine stitch. Pull up the gathering stitches on the sleeve cap so that it is the same length as the shirt armhole. With the right sides together, pin, baste, and machine stitch the sleeve in place, neatly evening out the gathers as necessary to fit.

5 With the right sides together and the seams matching, join the underarm seam and the shirt side seam in one continuous operation. Press the seam open.

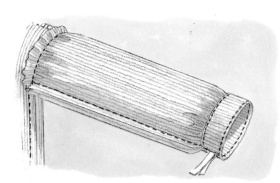

6 Turn up a 1in hem at the wrist edge of each sleeve and machine stitch in place. Stitch a second row close to the folded edge. Thread enough elastic through each hem to make the sleeve fit at the doll's wrist. Overlap the elastic at each end and hemstitch together to hold.

7 Make a narrow hem along the lower edge of the shirt and machine stitch across. Sew on the buttons where indicated on the pattern and then sew the two snaps where required, to fasten the center front.

Pants

8 To make the two pockets, turn under the seam allowances on the side and lower edges and machine stitch ¼in in from the edge. Turn under the top edge and stitch ½in in from the edge. Machine stitch the appropriate pocket to the front right leg and back left leg pieces as shown on the pattern, placing the wrong side of the pocket to the right side of the pants and stitching close to the edge.

9 With the right sides facing, stitch the two pants back and front pieces together at the center front. Clip the curved seam and press it open. Pin and baste the pleats in place at the waistline of the pants front pieces.

10 Pin the pants back and front pieces together with the right sides facing, and stitch the side seams up to the notch as marked on the pattern. Press the seams open. Make single hems at the side seam openings and along the back waistline. Finish the raw edges and baste in place.

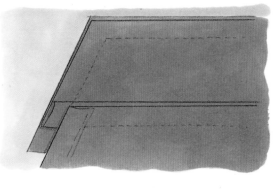

11 With the right sides facing, stitch the outer bib section to the pants front at the waistline. Press the seams upward. With right sides facing, stitch the two bib sections together around the outer edges. Clip across the corners, turn right side out and press. On the inside bib, turn in the remaining raw edge and hemstitch in place at the waistline.

12 To make the straps, fold each one lengthwise in half with the right sides together and machine stitch around leaving one short edge open. Turn right side out and topstitch close to the finished edges. Baste the straps in position at the back waistline as indicated on the pattern, and then stitch all the finished edges, making two rows of stitching at the back waistline to hold the straps firmly in place.

13 Turn up the pants bottoms to the required length and topstitch in place with two rows of machine stitching. Fix the two snaps to the bib front and the straps following the manufacturer's instructions.

Boots

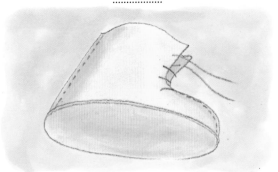

14 With the right sides outside, place the four boot sections together in pairs to make two boots. Pin, tack and machine stitch along the back seam and the front seam from the base of the foot to the notch as shown. Working on the wrong side, spread a fine line of glue along the edge of the base of the shoe and the sole. Bring the edges together and press firmly between the fingers until they are firmly attached. Thread the lace through holes in each boot using a strong needle and about 1yd of lace for each boot.

BOY'S BOWTIE AND HANKY

CLOTHING PATTERN PIECES
FOR GIRL

- Patterns for this project should be enlarged to twice the size. If you have access to a photocopier with an enlarging facility, set it to 200%. Otherwise, trace the patterns on a grid, following the procedure outlined on page 7. (See also the Checklist on page 99).

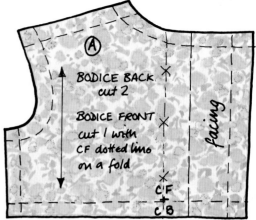

BODICE BACK
cut 2

BODICE FRONT
cut 1 with
CF dotted line
on a fold

facing

CF
CB

15 Cut two rectangles of fabric, one measuring 3in x 6in and the other 2in × 1¼in. Fold the larger one lengthwise in half with the right sides together and machine stitch together ¼in from the raw edge, leaving one short side open. Turn right side out and press. Fold the short ends under to meet in the center and overcast the edges together.

Other pattern pieces:
For both the underskirt and the dress skirt, cut a rectangle on the straight grain from each fabric:

Underskirt ⓖ   11 in x 36 in
Dress skirt ⓗ   10 in x 36 in
Dress frill ⓙ   1¾ in x 18 in

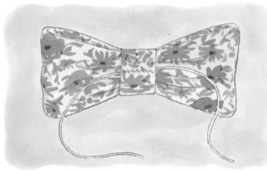

16 In the same way, fold, stitch, and turn the smaller rectangle of fabric. Wrap this around the center of the bow and overcast the ends together. Thread the elastic through the loop at the back of the bow and tie it around the doll's neck underneath the collar.

17 To make the hanky, machine stitch a narrow hem on all sides of the fabric square.

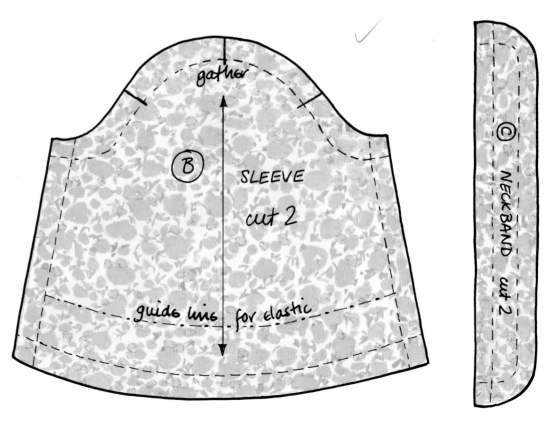

gather

Ⓑ SLEEVE

cut 2

guide line for elastic

Ⓒ NECKBAND cut 2

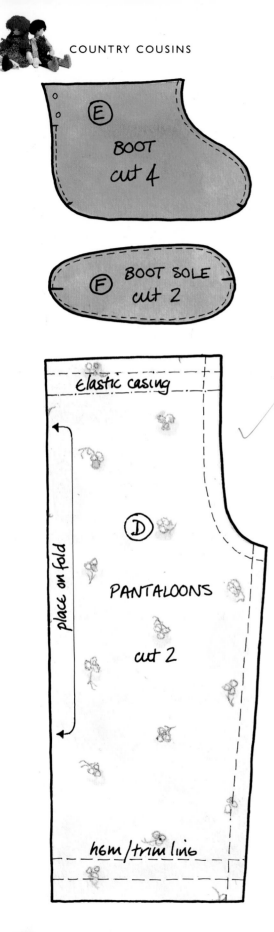

E BOOT cut 4

F BOOT SOLE cut 2

elastic casing

D

place on fold

PANTALOONS

cut 2

hem/trim line

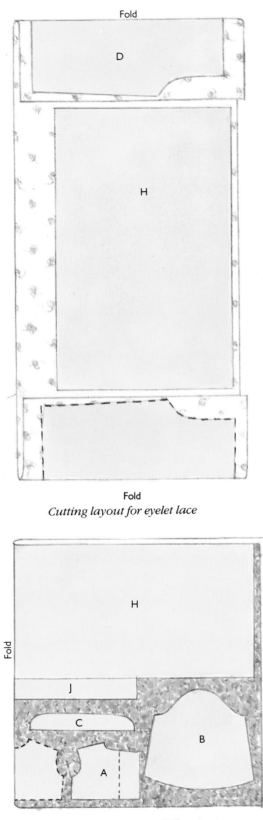

Fold

D

H

Fold

Cutting layout for eyelet lace

Fold

H

J

C

B

A

Cutting layout for small floral print

GIRL'S CLOTHES ~ PANTALOONS

1 Turn up the hem at the ankle, as indicated on the pattern, and baste in place. Pin and baste the trim to the wrong side of the hem and machine stitch across. With the right sides together, pin, baste, and machine stitch the inner leg seams of each piece to form a pair. Place one leg inside the other with right sides together; then pin, baste, and stitch around the center curved seam.

2 Turn under the seam allowance along the waist edge and stitch in place to form a casing for the elastic. Stitch a second row at the outside edge. On the wrong side, unpick one or two stitches in the first seam and thread about 10in of elastic through the casing. Adjust the length for the correct fit, overlap the ends, and overcast to secure.

UNDERSKIRT

3 Fold the skirt fabric in half widthwise, pin, baste, and stitch the center back seam. Press open. Turn up a ½in hem and baste in place. Baste the trim to the inside of the hem and then machine stitch through all thicknesses to secure, overlapping the seam at the back.

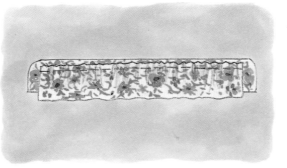

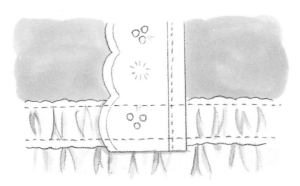

4 Make a ½in hem at the waist edge to form a casing, as for the pantaloons. Thread about 10in of elastic through the casing and adjust to fit. Cut two 8in lengths of trim for shoulder straps and pin in position at the waist 3in from each side of the center front and back. Adjust the length of the straps as required and machine stitch across.

DRESS

5 With the right sides facing, machine stitch the back and front shoulder seams together. Press the seams open. Fold the center back facings to the wrong side and baste in place. Fold the neck ruffle with right sides together, pin, baste, and stitch both short ends and then turn right side out. Run a row of machine gathering stitches on the neck seamline of the ruffle and pull up the gathers until the ruffle fits the neckband between the notches.

6 Pin and baste the ruffle to the outer neckband with the right sides together. Place the inner neckband on top of the ruffle also with right sides together and stitch along the seamline leaving the neck edge open. Turn the neckband to the right side and then pin and baste the outer neckband to the neckline of the bodice and stitch in place. Turn under the seam allowance of the inner neckband and hemstitch on the wrong side.

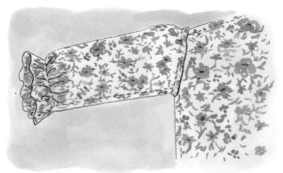

7 Gather the sleeve cap between the notches so that the sleeve fits the armhole. Baste in place, even out the gathers, and stitch around. Using shirring elastic in your machine, stitch around the guide line at the wrist and then finish the sleeve with a narrow hem. With right sides facing, pin, baste, and machine stitch the underarm and bodice side seams together in a continuous operation.

8 Make a row of gathering stitches along the skirt waistline. With right sides facing, stitch the center back seam to within 2½in of the waistline. Press the seam allowance to the wrong side of the opening. Pull up the gathering stitches so that the skirt fits the bodice waistline. With right sides facing, pin, baste, and machine stitch the skirt and bodice together. Turn under the facing and slipstitch to the inside of the waist seam.

9 Turn up a small hem on the skirt and machine stitch in place. Sew the four buttons to the center back left-hand side bodice, and attach the three snaps to secure the opening.

BOOTS

10 With the right sides facing, place the four boot sections together in pairs to make two boots. Pin, baste, and machine stitch along the center front seam and the back seam below the notch. In the same way, stitch the sole to the base of the boot with the right sides together and then turn it right side out. Thread a 16in length of braid through holes as indicated on the pattern. Pierce the holes with a leather punch or a large sewing needle. Tie a bow to finish.

CLASSIC RAG DOLL

For more experienced needleworkers, this beautiful doll presents an irresistible challenge. From her rosebud-patterned body to her lacy petticoats, beribboned dress and embroidered face, this doll is perfect in every detail.

It is worth taking time and care when choosing and buying fabrics – remember this doll is a masterpiece in the making and will be treasured for many years!

As with all the dolls, you don't have to copy the fabrics used in our example. Try mixing and matching different swatches of fabric and yarn .

*Pretty patterned
fabric for
the body*

*Navy polkadot dress fabric
and eyelet lace*

MATERIALS

DOLL (measures 24in high)

- 10in of 36in-wide plain cotton fabric such as muslin for body
- 10in of 36in-wide patterned fabric for the body
- 1yd of ½in-wide lace for trimming the seams
- 4oz ball of black knitting worsted for the hair
- 20in of 1in-wide red satin ribbon for hair bow
- Black, blue, and red stranded embroidery floss for facial features
- Loose synthetic stuffing or kapok

UNDERSKIRT AND PANTALOONS

- 1yd of 36in-wide white lawn
- 1yd of ½in-wide white satin ribbon for the belt
- 2yd of 2½in-wide white lace edging for the hem of the underskirt
- 1yd of 1in-wide white eyelet lace trim for the hem of the pantaloons
- 1yd of ½in-wide white lace for the bodice
- 6in of white elastic ¼in wide
- Three small snaps

DRESS

- 27in of 44in-wide navy and white polkadot cotton fabric for the dress
- 10in of white poplin for the collar and cuffs
- 16in of ½in-wide lace edging for the collar
- Three small snaps
- 2¼yd of ½in-wide white satin ribbon for the trim
- 1yd of ¾in-wide navy satin ribbon for the belt
- Bias binding to match dress fabric

SHOES

- 8in square of red felt
- 20in of narrow red cord to tie

STOCKINGS

- A pair of child's socks, smallest size, (striped or plain)

Plain white lawn and eyelet lace trimming

DOLL PATTERN PIECES

- Patterns for this project should be
- enlarged to twice the size. If you have
- access to a photocopier with an enlarging
- facility, set it to 200%. Otherwise, trace the
- patterns on a grid, following the
- procedure outlined on page 7.
- (See also the Checklist overleaf).

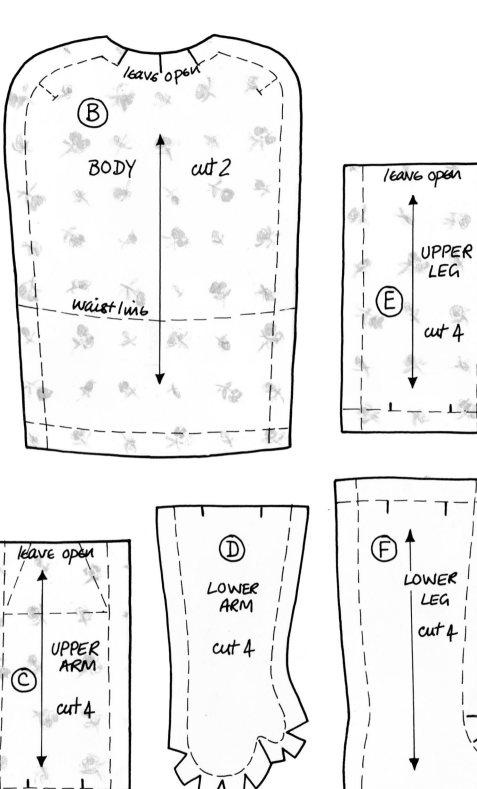

HEAD   cut 2

Ⓐ

leave open

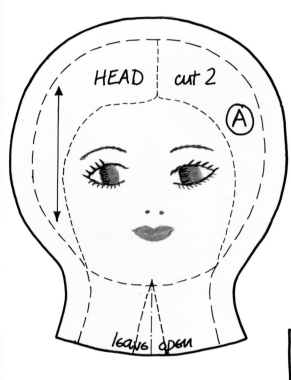

BODY   cut 2

Ⓑ

leave open

waistline

UPPER LEG

Ⓔ

cut 4

leave open

SOLE

Ⓖ

cut 2

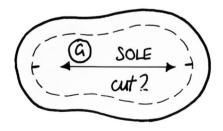

UPPER ARM

Ⓒ

cut 4

leave open

LOWER ARM

Ⓓ

cut 4

LOWER LEG

Ⓕ

cut 4

leave open

Fold

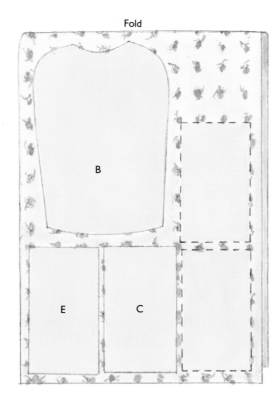

Cutting layout for tiny patterned fabric

Fold

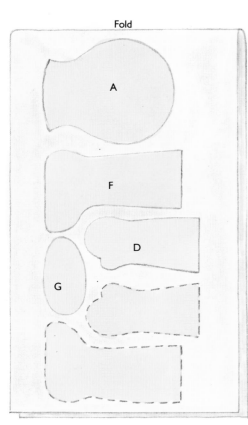

Cutting layout for muslin fabric

THE DOLL ~ BODY AND HEAD

1 With right sides together, and using machine stitching, join the back and front body pieces, leaving the neck edges open between the notches. Turn over the seam allowance at the neck and finger-press. Turn right side out and, with the help of a knitting needle, stuff evenly.

The classic rag doll showing the hand-sewn lace around the neck and seam joints of the arms and legs.

2 Using dressmakers' carbon paper, transfer the position and shape of the facial features lightly to the right side of one head piece.

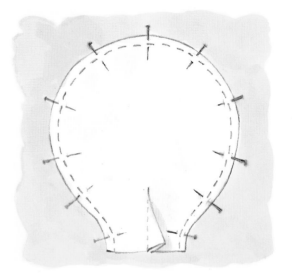

3 Pin, baste, and machine stitch the neck darts of both head pieces and then join them together, leaving the neck edge open. Turn to the right side and stuff evenly, as before.

4 Join the head to the body by inserting the neck into the body and, with matching sewing thread, hemstitch it in place, adjusting the neck length and stuffing as necessary.

ARMS

5 Join the upper arm pieces to the lower arm pieces matching the notches, and then join the completed pieces together to form a pair, leaving the top edge open as directed on the pattern piece. Trim the seam and carefully clip the curved seam allowance around the hand.

6 Turn the arms right side out and stuff to within 1in of the top. Turn in the top raw edge and make an inverted pleat on each side.

7 Pin the arms to the body at the shoulder line as indicated on the pattern, making sure you arrange the arms so that the thumbs are facing front. Using matching thread, firmly overcast in place.

LEGS

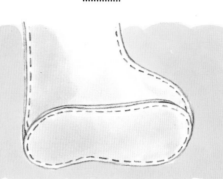

8 Join the upper leg pieces to the lower leg pieces, matching the notches, and then join the completed pieces together to form a pair, leaving the top and bottom edges open as directed on the pattern. Insert the sole into the base of the foot, matching the notches, then pin, baste, and machine stitch around.

9 Carefully clip the curved seams and turn the legs to the right side and stuff to within 1in of the top. Turn in the raw edge, and then pin and baste across with the seams at the center of the leg. Firmly overcast the legs to the body ½in in front of the base seam to allow the doll to sit down. Finally, handsew the lace around the neck and the seams on the arms and legs.

FACE

10 Using appropriate colors, embroider the eyes, nose, and mouth using stranded embroidery floss. Work the eyebrows in stem stitch using one strand of black. Then outline the eyes in stem stitch using two strands of black thread. Embroider the eyelashes in blanket stitch using one strand of black. And then fill in the pupils with satin stitch using two strands of black and the iris with two strands of blue.

11 Suggest the nostrils with two French knots using one strand of black thread. Fill in the lips using one strand of light red embroidery floss and satin stitch as shown. Then outline the mouth in stem stitch using one strand of deeper red.

12 Suggest the cheeks with a light dusting of blusher, practicing first on a scrap of fabric to get just the right depth of pink.

HAIR

13 Cut the yarn in to equal lengths 32in long. Using one of the lengths, tie the strands loosely together across the middle. Making this strand the center part, place the remaining strands over the head and sew them in place along the center dotted line. Allowing about 10-12 strands for the bangs, spread the remaining yarn over the head and sew it in place along the hairline at the neck.

14 Bring all these strands up again and, using the red satin ribbon, tie them with a bow on top of the head. Trim the ends of the ponytail evenly. The bangs can be trimmed straight across or the long strands of yarn can be twisted together in groups to form curls. Do this by tightly twisting together one or two strands until they begin to twist on themselves. Fold in half, then place the raw ends under the curl, which will form when the yarn is "doubled" over. With a spot of clear glue, stick the yarn ends firmly to the head.

CLOTHING PATTERN PIECES

- Patterns for this project should be enlarged to twice the size. If you have access to a photocopier with an enlarging facility, set it to 200%. Otherwise, trace the patterns on a grid, following the procedure outlined on page 7.
- (See also the Checklist on page 112).

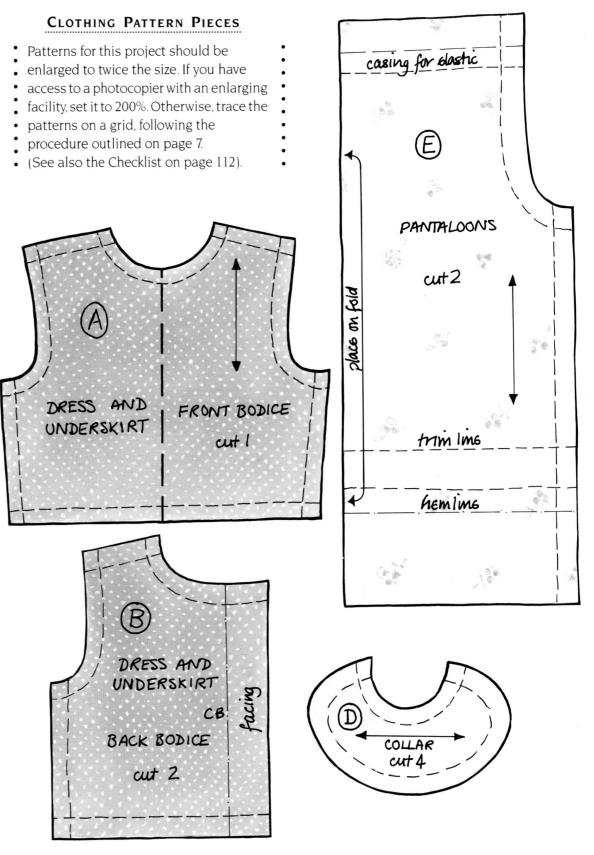

(A) DRESS AND UNDERSKIRT — FRONT BODICE cut 1

(B) DRESS AND UNDERSKIRT CB BACK BODICE cut 2 — facing

(D) COLLAR cut 4

(E) PANTALOONS cut 2 — casing for elastic — place on fold — trim line — hem line

Other pattern pieces:

From white lawn, cut the following rectangles on the straight grain.

Underskirt frills — one piece (H) 4¾in × 30in

two pieces (J) 7in × 30in

From white poplin, cut two cuff pieces (K) 2¼in × 5¾in

Cut one bias strip for the collar (L) 1in × 7in

From navy and white polkadot fabric, cut the dress skirt (M) 11½in. × 41in.

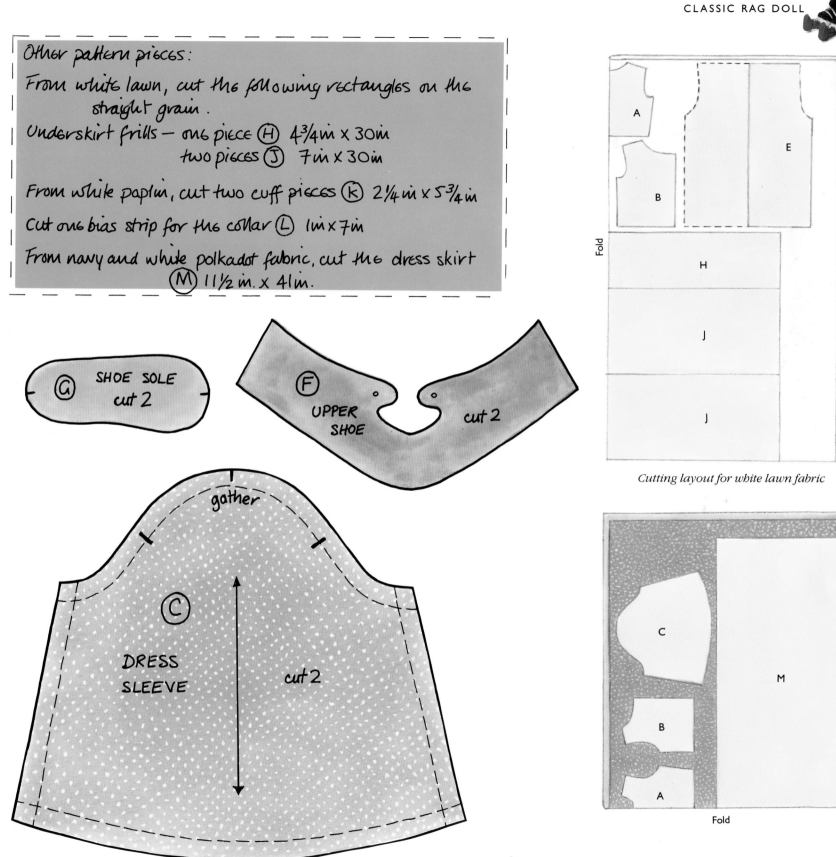

(G) SHOE SOLE cut 2

(F) UPPER SHOE cut 2

gather

(C) DRESS SLEEVE cut 2

Cutting layout for white lawn fabric

Cutting layout for navy and white polkadot fabric

Fold

Cutting layout for white poplin

THE CLOTHES ~ PANTALOONS

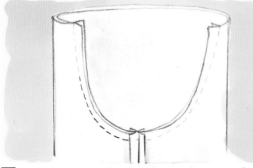

1 With the right sides inside, pin, baste, and machine stitch the inner leg seams of each piece to form a pair. Place one leg inside the other and join the two legs together along the center curved seam. Trim, clip into the curved seam, and pull one leg through.

2 Make a narrow double turning at the ankle on each leg and machine stitch across. Then, pin, baste, and machine stitch two decorative rows of lace trim as indicated on the pattern.

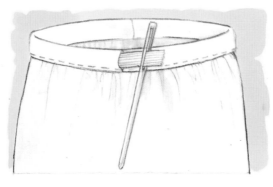

3 Make a double turning at the waist to form a casing for the elastic. Using an elastic threader or small safety pin, run the elastic through the casing by unpicking a few stitches on the wrong side, and adjust it for the correct fit. Tie the elastic securely and stitch to close.

UNDERSKIRT

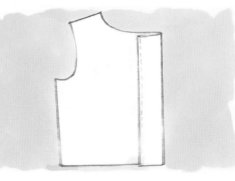

4 On each piece of the back bodice, fold in the center facing, pin, baste and sew in place.

5 Join the back and front bodice pieces together at the shoulder seams. Press the seams open. Then machine stitch a length of ½in-wide white satin ribbon (left over from the belt) along the center front. Apply two rows of narrow lace trim to each side, machine stitching them edge to edge for a neat finish. Cut out two or three flowers from the lace used to trim the body seams, and hand sew them to the center front, as shown in the diagram.

6 Turn in and baste the seam allowances around the edges of the neck and armholes. Covering the hems with the lace trim, pin, baste and machine stitch in place, overlapping the seams with a narrow hem at the underarm point.

7 Join the upper section of the underskirt with a center back seam about 1½in long. Finish the opening above to match the bodice opening at the center back.

8 With right sides together, join the side seams of the lower section of the underskirt. Press the seams open. Using a long stitch for gathering, run a row of stitching along the top edges of both underskirt sections.

9 Pull up the underside thread and gather the top edge of the upper section to fit the bodice waist, evening the gathers. Then pin, baste and machine stitch in place. In the same way, gather the bottom section to fit the lower edge of the upper section and stitch in place.

10 Turn up the hem, pin, and baste. Apply a row of lace trim, placing the straight edge just over the previous basting stitches. Pin, baste, and machine stitch to hold both the hem and trim in place.

11 Sew the snaps to the center back bodice opening. Stitch the narrow ribbon to the waist at the center back. In practice, this will cross and tie at the center front.

bias binding and then pin and hem it to the neck seam line. Turn the facings to the wrong side and press carefully.

20 Turn up the hem to the required length and, using matching thread, hem in place. Then sew snaps to the center back opening to fasten and complete the dress.

DRESS

12 With right sides together, begin by machine stitching the bodice backs to the bodice front at the shoulder seams. Trim to avoid bulky seams and press the seams open.

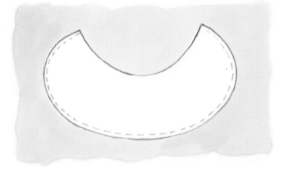

13 Construct the two collar sections by basting and machine sewing the pieces together (in pairs) along the outer curved edges. Trim and clip the seam, turn and press. Baste the lace trim in place along the outer edge and machine stitch.

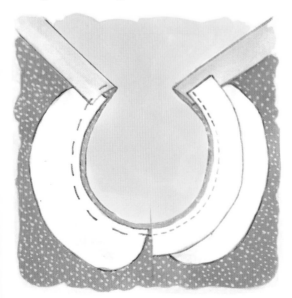

14 Baste both collars in place along the neck edge. Fold back the facing to the right side and then baste and machine stitch the bias binding along the seam line. Turn under the opposite edge of the

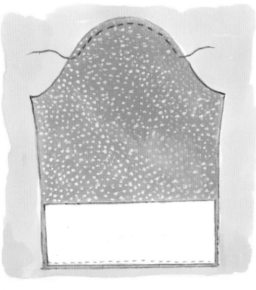

15 Gather the sleeve cap between the notches. Gather the lower edge of the sleeve to fit the longer edge of the cuff. With right sides together, baste and machine stitch in place.

16 With right sides together, pin, baste, and machine stitch the sleeves into the bodice armhole. Clip the curved seams. Join the side seams and the underarm seams together in one continuous seam. Then turn the cuffs in half to the wrong side. Press and fold and hem in place.

17 Machine stitch the trim onto the skirt, placing the first row 3in away from the lower raw edge and the second row 1in above.

18 Stitch the center back seam to within 3½in of the waistline. Turn under the raw edges of the opening, machine stitch to finish. and turn to the wrong side.

19 Following the instructions for making the underskirt, gather the waistline to fit the bodice. Pin, baste, and machine stitch in place, omitting gathers from the facing.

STOCKINGS

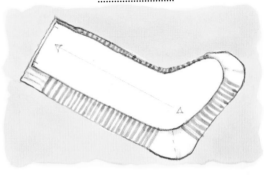

21 Turn the child's socks inside out and pin the lower leg pattern in place, matching the center front of the pattern to the front of the sock and the heel of the pattern to the heel of the sock.

22 With a pencil, draw around the pattern onto the sock and then machine stitch along the line using zigzag machine stitch. Trim the excess fabric and turn right side out. Repeat for second stocking.

SHOES

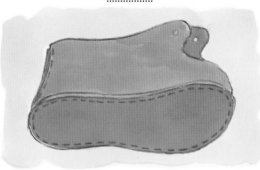

23 With matching thread and using ⅛in seam allowances throughout, machine stitch the center back seam of each upper shoe. Insert the sole into the base of the shoe, basting in place before machine stitching around. Leave the seams showing on the outside. Thread the narrow cord through the front straps to tie in a bow.

DEMONSTRATE YOUR DOLLMAKING SKILLS WITH THIS SOPHISTICATED AND

DECORATIVE LADY. SHE MAKES A VERY ATTRACTIVE SPECIAL GIFT FOR AN OLDER

CHILD, TEENAGER, OR ADULT - THAT IS, IF YOU CAN BEAR TO GIVE HER AWAY

ONCE YOU HAVE MADE HER!

BUTTON & BEAD DOLL

Button and bead joints make this doll a fascinating example of the dollmaker's art. Carefully postioned beads create knee and elbow joints and mean that the doll will sit gracefully on a shelf, desk, or chair.

Buttons have been used to attach the legs to the body, and thick thread attaches the arms – allowing them to move freely. The body is made in brightly patterned fabrics so that attaching a matching skirt and sleeves is quick to do and gives a striking overall effect.

Take special care with the face. Use the ingenious technique of tracing the features on the reverse of the face fabric and you will get perfect results.

*Fabric for
arms*

*Dress
fabric*

*Fabric for
legs*

*Bodice
fabric*

MATERIALS

DOLL (measures 17in high)

- 8in × 10in of cotton fabric (or muslin) for the head, neck, and shoulders
- 11in × 10in of small gingham check cotton fabric for the top bodice and body
- 6in × 8in of harmonizing solid-color cotton fabric for the arms
- 12in × 16in of striped cotton fabric (in harmonizing colors) for the legs
- Four wooden macrame beads, ⅝in across with ¼in-wide holes, for the elbow and knee joints (if beads are not available, the joints can be made by gathering the fabric).
- Two buttons, ½in across with two holes, for the hip joints
- 1oz of thin yarn for the hair, either knitting yarn or tapestry yarn in a single color or various shades of the same color
- Synthetic stuffing or kapok
- Long darning needle
- Pencil, or preferably an air-vanishing pencil for tracing on light fabric
- Dressmaker's chalk or yellow or silver marking pencil for tracing on dark fabrics
- Brown or black fine-point permanent ink fabric pen or waterproof felt pen for drawing the face details
- Acrylic or fabric paints in white, black, brown, red, yellow, and blue for filling in the face details
- Fine paintbrushes
- Acrylic varnish or white craft glue for sealing the paint
- Seam sealant, optional

DRESS

- 12in of 36in-wide contrasting patterned cotton fabric for the skirt and sleeves

DECORATION

- Embroidery threads and very fine ribbons for the shoe laces, bracelet, and hair decorations
- Enough ⅛in glass seed beads for the necklace and eight similar beads for the shoes

*Muslin for
the body, and
threads and fine ribbon for detailing*

*Buttons
for the
hip joints*

*Glass seed
beads*

*Macramé
beads for elbow
and knee joints*

*Embroidery threads
in shades of russet and
brown for the hair*

DOLL PATTERN PIECES

Patterns for this project are full size and do not need to be enlarged. The body piece is shown overleaf. Before pinning on the pieces, also see the Checklist overleaf.

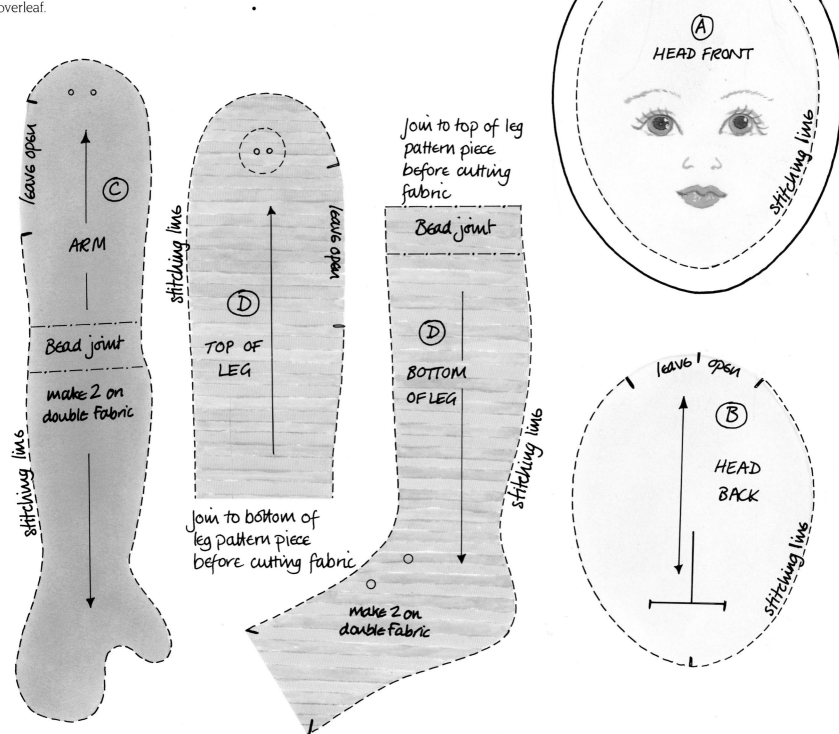

leave open

(A)
HEAD FRONT

stitching line

leave open

(C)

ARM

Bead joint

make 2 on double Fabric

stitching line

stitching line

(D)

TOP OF LEG

leave open

Join to bottom of leg pattern piece before cutting fabric

Join to top of leg pattern piece before cutting fabric

Bead joint

(D)

BOTTOM OF LEG

stitching line

make 2 on double Fabric

leave open

(B)

HEAD BACK

stitching line

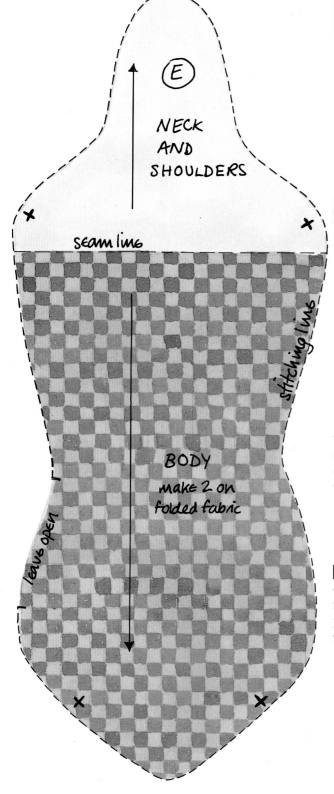

E

NECK
AND
SHOULDERS

seam line

stitching line

BODY

make 2 on
folded fabric

leave open

CHECKLIST

- Trace off the outline of the actual size pattern pieces. Transfer all marks and cut out, see pages 6-7.
- The body, arm and leg patterns show the stitching line only and seam allowances are added after stitching.
- Do not cut out the fabric pieces until instructed to do so.
- Press all fabrics: washing is optional as this doll is purely decorative.
- Set your sewing machine to the required stitch, check the length and tension and do a test run on your chosen fabric, see page 8.
- Use seam sealant sparingly on clipped curved seams to prevent fraying.
- Before painting the face details, test your paint on a spare piece of fabric.

THE DOLL ~

Note: the doll is made up in an unorthodox way whereby many of the doll pattern pieces show the stitching line only. Follow the instructions carefully, observing that these pieces are stitched first and then cut out.

BODY

1 Cut a piece of cotton (or muslin) fabric, 4in × 10in wide and a piece of checked bodice fabric, 7in x 10in wide. With the right sides together, pin and machine stitch along one long edge. Press the seam allowances toward the patterned fabric.

Care and attention to detail are a feature of the front and back of the doll.

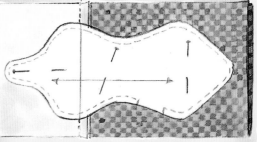

2 Fold the fabric widthwise in half with the right sides together and seams matching. Place the body pattern centrally on the fabric, aligning the seam line on the paper with the seam line on the fabric, and allowing for ¼in seams. Pin the pattern in place and draw around the outline.

3 Using matching sewing threads for each of the two fabrics, machine stitch around the body, leaving the opening as indicated on the pattern. Run a second line of machine stitching just outside the first one around the neck and shoulders to strengthen the seam.

4 Cut out the body adding a ¼in seam allowance all around. Clip the curved seams and use seam sealant if desired. Turn to the right side. Stuff very firmly, especially the neck area. Use a knitting needle to help push the filling in place. Overcast the opening to close.

ARMS

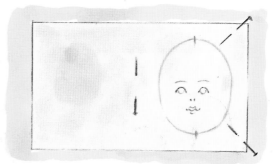

5 Fold the cotton fabric for the arms widthwise in half. Trace around the arm pattern and repeat for the second arm, allowing for ¼in seams all around. Stitch as for the body. Make one or two horizontal stitches between the thumb and hand, for easy turning.

6 Cut out the arms, trimming back the ¼in seam allowance to ⅛in around the hand and thumb. Clip the curved seam allowances and apply seam sealant to the hand area. Turn to the right side.

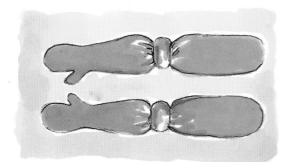

7 Stuff the thumb first with tiny wisps of filling. Then stuff the hand fairly flat; begin to stuff more firmly at the wrist and continue with the lower arm until the first bead line as marked on the paper pattern. Roll the upper-arm fabric lengthwise and slip it through the wooden bead, pushing the bead down against the stuffing. If wooden beads are not available, run a gathering stitch along the elbow line, pull gathers, and knot firmly. Repeat for the second arm, make sure that both elbows are evenly positioned. Stuff the upper arms a little less firmly. Using matching thread, close the opening.

LEGS

8 From the leg fabric, cut a piece measuring 12in × 14in, making sure the stripes will run horizontally across the leg. Fold in half, with the right sides together, and draw around the pattern twice, as for the arms. Machine stitch around, leaving the two openings as indicated on the pattern.

9 Cut out the legs, adding ¼in seam allowances. Clip into the curved seam between the leg and foot. Working on the wrong side, open out the foot area and fold flat, bringing the seams together in the centre. Mark a curved line for the toes as indicated in the illustration, pin, and machine stitch. Trim the seam to ¼in and turn right side out.

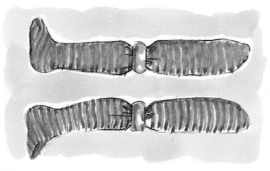

10 Stuff the feet first, pushing the filling into all the corners with a knitting needle. Continue to stuff the lower leg up to the knee firmly. Slip beads on as indicated for the arm joints. Stuff the top of the leg firmly and close the opening with slipstitch.

HEAD AND FACE

11 From the remaining cotton (or muslin) fabric, cut a rectangle measuring 4in × 8in. Place the face pattern on the wrong side of one half of the fabric, leaving the other half for the back of the head. Trace around the oval shape only with the vanishing pen. Mark the top and bottom positioning lines.

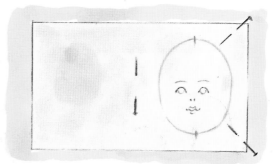

12 With the wrong side up, place the face pattern under the fabric; align the positioning marks and pin to secure. Working against a window pane or on a lightbox, trace the features through to the wrong side of the fabric using a pencil. Remove the paper pattern.

13 Place the face fabric with the traced features on white paper where the lines drawn on the reverse side should be clearly distinguishable on the right side of the fabric.

14 With the brown permanent ink pen, carefully retrace the features on the right side of the fabric – the pupil can be suggested in black. Notice that the eyebrows are drawn with short strokes, rather than one continuous line.

PAINTING THE FACE

Note: always wait for the paint to dry thoroughly before applying further coats or adjacent colors.

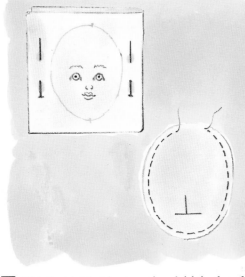

15 With the right sides together, fold the face fabric in half and pin to secure. Machine stitch around ¼in inside the marked outline leaving the opening at the top, as shown on the pattern. Cut out just inside the marked line. Place the back head pattern on the back head fabric. Transfer the positioning mark for attaching the head to the body.

16 Turn through to the right side. Stuff very firmly, smoothing out any creases along the curved edges. Neatly overcast the opening to close.

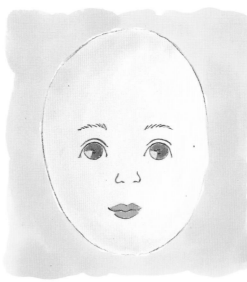

17 Begin by painting in the iris. Paint three-quarters of it, then add white to the eye color and paint the "half past to quarter to" section of the iris in the lighter color.

19 With white paint, lightly touch up the corners of the eyes outside the iris and put a highlight on each eye by painting a dot on the top right-hand quarter of each eye.

20 Finally, to seal and protect the paint, and also to add shine to the features, paint a layer of acrylic varnish or white craft glue on the eyes and mouth. This looks milky when wet, but it will dry clear.

SOFT SCULPTURE

A few "soft sculpture" stitches strategically placed give the face that degree of expression.

18 Then paint the mouth a pinky red and leave to dry. Add white to the lip color to make it lighter and paint the upper part of the lower lip. Paint the pupil black. Using the brown pen, go over the top line of the eyes to make them thicker.

21 With the darning needle threaded with doubled strong thread, start at the back of the head and sink the eye corners by taking a minute stitch at each

eye corner. Make a second stitch at each point, pulling gently but not too tightly to get the desired effect. Make one stitch under the lower lip to get a chin effect, and knot securely at the back.

ASSEMBLING THE DOLL

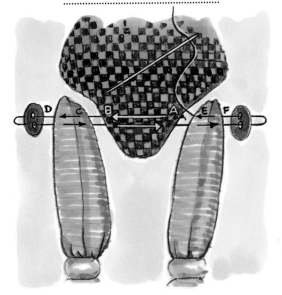

22 Thread the darning needle with doubled strong thread and, following the diagram, begin by joining the legs to the body as follows. Insert the needle at point A, and bring it out at point B. Repeat at point C and D. Bring the needle out through one hole of the button and insert it again through the second hole. Return the needle through points D, C, B, and A. Insert it again at E and bring it out at F. Attach the button as before and return the needle through points F and E. Repeat twice again until the stitching feels firm. Make a knot at a convenient hidden point such as A or B.

The hair can be decorated with tiny braids, ribbons, and beads.

23 Using doubled strong thread, join the arms to the body. Make the first stitch at the shoulder and a second stitch at the top of the arm. Repeat three or four times. Wind the thread around the stitches between the body and the arm, and work about three buttonhole stitches to secure the joint. Stitch through the body and the arm once more, and finally secure the thread hiding the end inside the body. Repeat for the second arm.

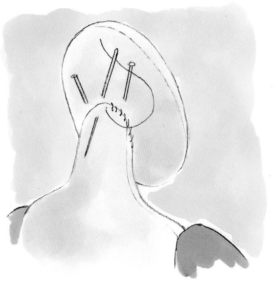

24 To join the head to the body, first cut through the fabric on the back of the head along the shape mark using small, sharp-pointed scissors. To make space for the neck, remove a small amount of filling as necessary. Push the neck into the space with a turning movement and position the head as desired, straight or slightly inclined to one side. Make a narrow turning on the cut edges, pin in place, and overcast the head to the neck, stitching twice for a firm attachment.

HAIR

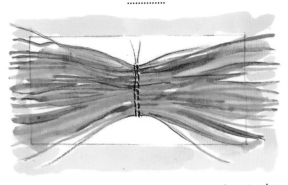

25 On a piece of paper, draw a line 2½in long in the center, parallel to the short edge. Cut 16in lengths of yarn and lay them across the line until there are enough to make a nice head of hair; the center of the strands should be on the pencil line. Machine stitch twice through the yarn and paper along the line, which will form the center part; secure the ends of the machine stitching firmly. Tear off the paper.

26 Pin the hair on the head, placing one end of the seam above the face at the center hairline point, and the other end at the center back neckline. Adjust if necessary, and backstitch in place. Arrange the hair to cover the back of the neck; comb out with the fingers and trim to an even length. Embellish with ribbons or embroidery threads tied or plaited into her hair.

CLOTHING PATTERN PIECES

Patterns for this project are full size and do not need to be enlarged. Before pinning on the pattern pieces, see the Checklist on page 122.

THE CLOTHES ~ SKIRT

1 From the skirt fabric cut a rectangle measuring 8½in × 24in. Join the short edges right sides together, pin, and machine stitch. Press the seams open. Make a double hem ⅜in deep and machine stitch in place.

Other pattern pieces:

For the skirt, cut a rectangle 8in × 24in from patterned cotton fabric.

For the bodice, cut a rectangle 4in × 8in from the small checked cotton.

For the waistband, cut a length measuring 3in × 9in from fabric to match the skirt.

2 Using a long machine stitch, run a line of gathering stitches along the waist edge of the skirt. Pull up the gathers and fit the skirt on the doll. Secure the threads, even out the gathers, and pin the skirt in place. Backstitch to the doll, stitching through the gathered line.

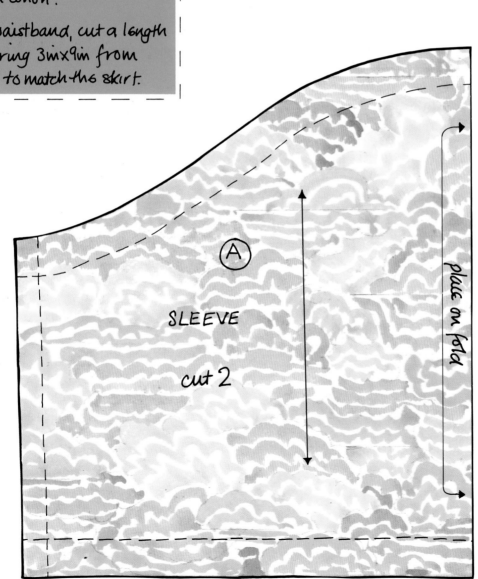

(A)

SLEEVE

cut 2

place on fold

SHOES

3 For the waistband, cut a length of skirt fabric measuring 9in × 3½in. Machine stitch a ¼in hem on both short sides. With the wrong sides together, fold lengthwise in half and press, open up and fold each half toward the center and press again. Pin together and topstitch around all four edges. Place on the waist to cover the raw edges of skirt, crossing over the ends at the back. Pin and stitch to the skirt.

SLEEVES

6 Stitch four beads on each of the feet where indicated, and thread a length of a thin ribbon or thick embroidery thread around them crossing in front as for laceup shoes. Tie in a bow to finish.

NECKLACE AND BRACELET

7 Thread the remaining small beads onto a short length of embroidery thread, to make a necklace about 5in long, and tie around the doll's neck, finishing with a bow at the back. Make the bracelet by tying a length of very narrow ribbon or thick embroidery thread around the doll's wrist.

BODICE TOP

The sleeves and skirt are gathered and stitched straight onto the body.

4 From the remaining bodice fabric, cut a rectangle measuring 8in × 4in. With the fabric right side down, fold the long edges inward so that it is about 1¾in wide. Press. Using double thread, run a central gathering line across the width. Pull up the gathers and secure the thread. Pin the bodice top in place with the gathers to the center front. Overlap the edges of the back and neatly hemstitch to close.

5 Cut out two sleeves from the remaining skirt fabric. With the right sides facing, pin and machine stitch the two short edges together. Press the seam open and turn right side out. Run a machine gathering line along both long edges, ¼in from the edge. Pull up the gathers on the sleeve cap, turn under the raw edge, and fit the sleeve on the doll with the underarm seam below the arm. Pin in place and overcast the sleeve to the doll at the shoulder. Pull up the gathers at the bottom of the sleeve, turn under the raw edge, and hand stitch the sleeve to the arms, just above the bead joint. Repeat for the second sleeve.

STITCH GLOSSARY

The following instructions explain in detail how to work the various stitches which are involved in making the doll projects.

Backstitch can be used for hand sewing a seam or a decorative embroidery stitch.

Bring the thread through on the stitch line, then make a small backward stitch to the right. Pass the needle forward under the fabric and bring it out one stitch length ahead, ready to make the next stitch. Make all the stitches the same length.

Blanket stitch gives a decorative finish to the edge of a garment.

Working from left to right, bring the needle out on the bottom line. Insert it above (the required depth of the stitch away) just to the right and bring it out immediately below, with the needle over the working thread. Continue in the same way making the stitches and the spaces between the same size, and keeping the purled edge of the stitch on the outer edge of the fabric.

Slit buttonhole: the raw edges are finished with buttonhole stitch.

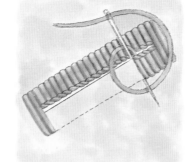

First run small stitches around the slit to the depth of both rows of buttonholing. Make two straight stitches at one end and, working from right to left, bring the thread out through the slit. Insert the needle from behind and bring it out just below the outline stitches with the thread under the needle. Take the thread back to the top edge and continue in this way to the end of the slit. Work one or two straight stitches across the end, turn the buttonhole around and complete the second side.

Chain stitch is a decorative embroidery stitch used for outlining and solid infilling.

Bring out the thread on the stitch line and hold it down to the left. Insert the needle at the starting point and bring it out a short distance below with the

thread under the needle. Pull the needle through to form the first chain and repeat the stitch along the line.

Feather stitch is a decorative embroidery stitch used for outlines and borders.

Bring the needle out on the stitch line and, with the thread held to the left, insert it a little way down to the right. Bring it out again directly below the starting point. Make a similar stitch to the left, on the same level, and continue working these two stages alternately.

French knots can be used singly to suggest nostrils and other face details as well as decorative stitch borders.

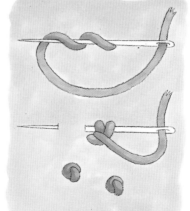

Bring out the thread where the knot is to be worked. Hold it down with the left thumb and, with the needle, encircle the thread twice. Twist the needle back to the

starting point and insert it close to where the thread emerged. Pull the needle through to the back and repeat as needed.

Gathering stitches can be made either by machine or hand.

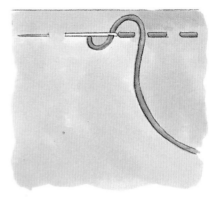

Sewing machine: lengthen the straight sewing stitch as required. Stitch and then pull up the lower thread to form the gathers. Knot firmly to secure.
Hand: with a long length of sewing thread in the needle make small- to medium-size running stitches along the entire length of the line to be gathered. Pull up as needed. It is important to begin with sufficient thread as knots will not allow the fabric to gather.

Hem stitch (hemming stitch) can be used to secure all types of hem by hand.

With the hem tacked in place, bring out the thread on the wrong side. Holding the needle at a diagonal take a tiny stitch in the fabric first and then insert it upward to take a small stitch in the hem fold. Pull through and repeat spacing the stitches evenly about 3/16 in apart.

Herringbone stitch can be used in embroidery or as a catch stitch to hold facings in place.

Working from left to right, make a small horizontal stitch in the upper layer of fabric, then a small horizontal stitch in the lower layer diagonally across the first stitch. Continue in this way keeping the thread loose.

Long and short stitch is used as a filling stitch in embroidery.

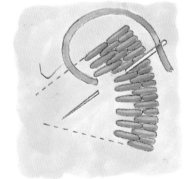

Work the first row in alternate long and short straight stitches following the outline of the area to be filled. Work the next and subsequent rows in straight stitches of equal length.

Overcasting (whipstitch) is used to close an opening and to join two separate sections such as attaching a limb to the body of a doll.

Working from right to left, take the needle diagonally over the edges of the fabric, picking up a few fabric threads only, and bring it through to the front again. Repeat as needed making small evenly spaced diagonal stitches.

Satin stitch is an infilling stitch used in embroidery.

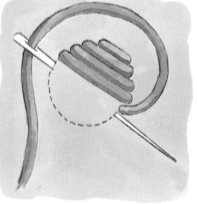

Working from the bottom left to the top right, embroider straight stitches diagonally across the area to be filled. The stitches should fit close together, all at the same angle and should form straight outside edges.

Slip stitch is used to join a folded edge to another fold or single layer of fabric. It is almost invisible since the larger part of each stitch is concealed within the fabric.

Working from right to left, bring the needle through on the fold, take it over into the fabric below (or into the opposite fold) picking up a single thread. Return the needle into the first folded edge and bring it out a short distance away. Repeat as needed.

Stem stitch is a line stitch used in embroidery.

Bring the needle out on the stitch line. Working from left to right, hold the thread down with the left thumb and make a small stitch to the right bringing the needle out a short distance toward the left. Repeat along the stitch line making the stitch at a slight angle to the stitch line to produce a broad twisted effect.

Stretch machine stitch is used for seaming stretch fabrics.

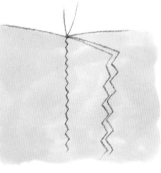

While some sewing machines have a special stitch, ordinary zigzag stitch will do the job just as well. Use the narrowest stitch, and do a test run to make sure it will "give" with the fabric.

Basting is used to temporarily hold together two or more fabric layers during the construction of a project.

Working from right to left, take several evenly spaced stitches onto the needle before pulling through. Use smaller even tacking stitches in areas that require close control and use longer uneven tacking stitches for general purposes such as during permanent stitching.

Zigzag stitch is a wide decorative border stitch used in embroidery.

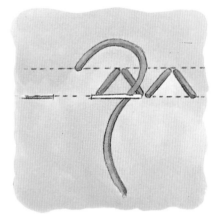

Bring the needle out on the upper stitch line. Working from right to left, insert the needle on the lower stitch line a short distance to the right. Making a horizontal stitch to the left, bring the needle out on the lower line a short distance beyond the level of the starting point. Reinsert the needle into the starting point and make a similar stitch on the top stitch line. Continue to the end of the row repeating the sequence.

INDEX

USEFUL ADDRESSES

International mail order addresses for general doll-making supplies.
Catalog available on request

United States
A Dollmaker's Marketplace
P.O. Box 110280
Campbell
CA 95011
Telephone: 1/800/328-3655

Australia
Sarah Sey Dolls and Crafts
39 Annangrove Road
Kenthurst
New South Wales 2156
Telephone/facsimile: (02) 6542181

United Kingdom
Children's Treasures
17 George Street
Hastings
East Sussex
TN34 3EG
Telephone/facsimile: (0424) 444117

Pick N' Choose
The Craft People
56 Station Road
Northwich
Cheshire
CW9 5RB
Telephone: (0606) 41523

GRID B